W9-CKR-847

BACKROADS

of

PENNSYLVANIA

EUCLID PUBLIC LIBRARY
631 EAST 222ND STREET
EUCLID, OH 44123
(216) 261-5300

BACKROADS

—of—

PENNSYLVANIA

Your Guide to Pennsylvania's Most
Scenic Backroad Adventures

TEXT BY MARCUS SCHNECK

PHOTOGRAPHY BY GLENN DAVIS

Voyageur Press

A Pictorial
Discovery Guide

DEDICATION

This book is dedicated to my son, Casey, who shared many of the trips described here with me, and to my wife, Jill Caravan, who kept the home fires burning while we satisfied our wanderlust.

—MS

To my wife Darlene for her infinite patience and loving support.

—GD

Text copyright © 2003 by Marcus Schneck
Photographs copyright © 2003 by Glenn Davis

All rights reserved. No part of this work may be reproduced or used in any form by any means—graphic, electronic, or mechanical, including photocopying, recording, taping, or any information storage and retrieval system—without written permission of the publisher.

Edited by Margret Aldrich
Designed by Andrea Rud
Cover and maps designed by JoDee Mittlestadt
Printed in China

03 04 05 06 07   5 4 3 2 1

Library of Congress Cataloging-in-Publication Data
Schneck, Marcus.
   Backroads of Pennsylvania : your guide to Pennsylvania's most scenic backroad adventures / text by Marcus Schneck ; photography by Glenn Davis.
       p. cm.
   ISBN 0-89658-550-6 (pbk. : alk. paper)
   1. Pennsylvania—Tours. 2. Scenic byways—Pennsylvania—Guidebooks.
   3. Automobile travel—Pennsylvania—Guidebooks. I. Davis, Glenn, 1954–
   II. Title.
   F147.3 .S355 2003
   917.4804'44—dc21

                            2003000029

Distributed in Canada by Raincoast Books, 9050 Shaughnessy Street, Vancouver, B.C. V6P 6E5

Published by Voyageur Press, Inc.
123 North Second Street, P.O. Box 338, Stillwater, MN 55082 U.S.A.
651-430-2210, fax 651-430-2211
books@voyageurpress.com
www.voyageurpress.com

Educators, fundraisers, premium and gift buyers, publicists, and marketing managers: Looking for creative products and new sales ideas? Voyageur Press books are available at special discounts when purchased in quantities, and special editions can be created to your specifications. For details contact the marketing department at 800-888-9653.

TITLE PAGE:

The sky clears over lush Amish farmland just after a thunderstorm.

TITLE PAGE, INSET:

Yellow lady slipper orchids grow on state game lands near Lebanon.

CONTENTS

INTRODUCTION

If you can't find it in Pennsylvania, you might want to question if it's worth looking for in the first place.

Whether you seek remnants from the very soul of our nation's history, timeless and massive geologic formations, or wildlife populations seemingly without end, a backroad somewhere in the Keystone State will take you to it. I promise you this, based on my more than two decades as a freelance travel and outdoors writer specializing in Pennsylvania. I've been there and back, through nearly every remote and not-so-remote corner of the state.

A trek through Pennsylvania is a trip worth making again and again, since the scenic surroundings are constantly changing. The shoreline of Sugar Lake in Erie National Wildlife Refuge is different from season to season, as are the view from Little Round Top at Gettysburg and the remote west-rim vista down into northern Pennsylvania's Pine Creek Gorge.

Some of the thirty-five backroads presented in this book, such as the drive through the little-known community of vacation homes on the non-touristy western side of Lake Wallenpaupack in the Poconos, were discovered on purposeful ventures to become familiar with a particular region. Other routes—like through the Buffalo Valley in Mifflin County, with its many references to bison in names of businesses, roadways, streams, and more—were lucky chance-encounters that immediately found their way into my mental store of favorite places.

Nature, scenery, and history—and sometimes just a unique or quirky aspect of a place—guided the choice of routes included here. If a spot offered something

FACING PAGE:

Buggy tracks run through fresh snow in southeastern Pennsylvania's Lancaster County.

ABOVE:

Icicles form on a farm fence near Millersburg on a chilly winter morning.

out of the ordinary for the casual passerby and had not been widely recognized, it gained a few extra points in the selection process. Parks with special features, sites of lesser-known history, and locales of true wilderness have become essential components of my wanderings, and of this book.

Even the most experienced Pennsylvania traveler will discover new aspects of the state in these pages. Much of the vast public holding in state parks, state forests, state game lands, and wildlife areas have gone largely unsung. For example, relatively few people, other than local residents, know of the view down into an active bald eagle nest offered by the overlook at Susquehannock State Park.

None of these trips totally escapes the influence of my lifelong love affair with wildlife. Pennsylvania offers an incredible diversity of wildlife that can be seen from the roadside, including bald eagles, bears, bluebirds, elks, herons, porcupines, otters, and hundreds of other species. Plant life is equally diverse, from old-growth hemlock forests near State College to vast wetland ecosystems in the Poconos and even an unexpected bit of prairie in the northwest.

In Pennsylvania, details of local history have often been overshadowed by the immense events of national history that transpired here, such as the Battle of Gettysburg and George Washington's crossing of the Delaware River. In fact, the deep and lasting footprint left on whole regions of the state by the logging and mining industries of the eighteenth and nineteenth centuries, and the "Great Leaving" during the last Native American uprisings, are generally mere footnotes in the average Pennsylvanian's historical knowledge base. These trips will examine some of that forgotten history.

This means the backroads you are about to explore tend to push along routes not detailed in most travel guides. That's only a tendency and not a cast-in-stone rule, however. Some also pass through well-known tourist destinations and along heavily traveled roadways, but always as part of the total experience. Never one to avoid "tourist traps," urban life, and heavy traffic, if it was all part of gaining access to someplace special, I've naturally included a healthy dose of such spots when appropriate. At times, unique tourist destinations, like the historic railroad district of Jim Thorpe, helped to decide a turn in a route or the overall length of a trek.

Some routes follow paved state highways, while others take you over unpaved dirt roads—a bit bumpy at times but always passable. Here and there, you will even encounter a one-lane bridge or an option to drive right through a small stream.

Specific times of year when travel is prime are indicated for some routes. For example, if you read a discussion about wildflowers and butterflies along a backroad, that route has more to offer in the late spring and summer than in the late fall and winter. Mentions of waterfowl migrations, on the other hand, indicate a preference for travel later in the year.

All routes are doable in a day or less. For some trips, one day allows for a thorough experience. For many others, a single day would mean sacrificing many of the stops and side-trips, along with the uniqueness they offer. The reader's own preferences, goals, and timetable can be the ultimate guide.

It might be advisable to pack camping gear. None of our backroads are completely without hotel or motel, or within ready access of those more civilized accommodations, but a great many of our routes lead to campgrounds. For camper or lodger, a detailed map, like DeLorme's *Pennsylvania Atlas and Gazetteer,* is essential to any Pennsylvania traveler's arsenal, as are binoculars, camera, and journal.

The backroads in these pages are at once a detailed guide to fascinating parts of the Keystone State and a more general demonstration of the largely undiscovered wealth waiting to be mined like a seam of the coal region's anthracite. Within a mile or two of every one of this book's backroads—and even intersecting these routes—lies another backroad with its own unique blend of place, people, and nature. In addition to leading the traveler to the state's hidden treasures, the routes described here can serve as a "how-to," encouraging adventurous travelers to set out in search of their own special backroads of Pennsylvania.

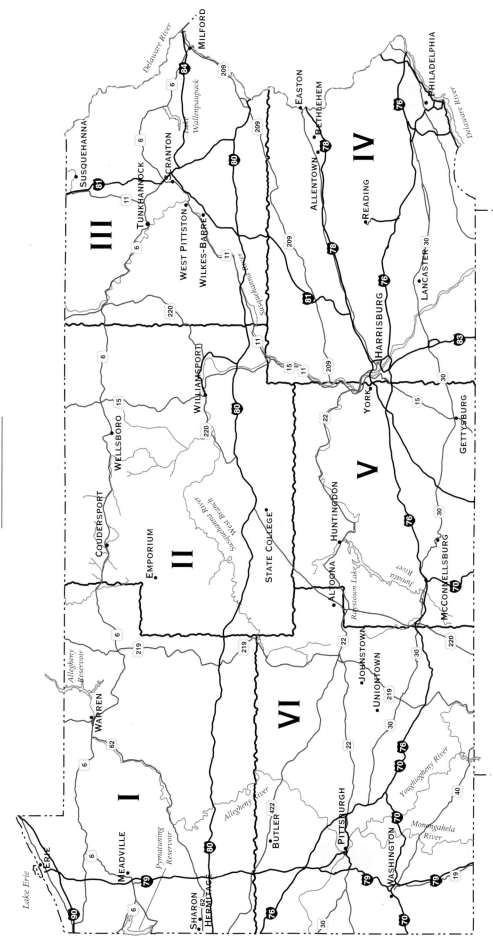

Numbers I–VI indicate the regions covered in each section of the book.

PART I

BIG FORCES ON THE LAND: THE NORTHWEST

FACING PAGE:

A locomotive traverses McKean County's Kinzua Bridge, which offers majestic views on clear, autumn days.

ABOVE:

A red maple leaf rests on yellow ferns in the Allegheny National Forest. The ANF is one of the only remaining large tracts of forestland that once covered much of the eastern United States.

The story of northwestern Pennsylvania is largely one of four major natural forces, their impact on the land, and their impact on the people and communities of the region.

Those undeniable forces include the Big Woods of the Allegheny National Forest; an expanse of scattered wetlands, lakes, and ponds; the flat coastal plain leading down to the shores of Lake Erie; and the waters of the Great Lake itself. Inside each of these zones are the stories of the industries the natural forces have created—such as logging and oil—the changing fortunes of those industries, and the people whose lives have been directed and altered forever by the environment that surrounds them.

The region provides many wonders to explore. It is home to Pennsylvania's only true coastline, the slip of land that just might be the state's most diverse wildlife habitat, vast tracts of forest, huge manmade lakes, and part of a roadway that *National Geographic* magazine described as one of America's most scenic drives.

THE LAKE ERIE SHORELINE
HIGHWAY 5 AND PRESQUE ISLE

THE ROUTE

From the Ohio state line at Pennsylvania's northwestern border, take West Lake Road east to get on Pennsylvania Highway 5. Follow Highway 5 northeast along the Lake Erie shore, diverting north on Pennsylvania Highway 832 to Presque Isle. Return to Highway 5 and continue to the New York state line.

Our first route is dominated by a single feature—Lake Erie, Pennsylvania's only Great Lake—and explores the landscape that nature and man have created under the influence of the massive body of water.

Lake Erie is the farthest south, fourth largest in area, and smallest in volume of the five Great Lakes. Its surface area is 9,910 square miles, but the lake averages just 62 feet in depth, with 210 feet being its deepest point. Lying between Lake Huron and Lake Ontario, Lake Erie receives water from Lake Huron through the St. Clair and Detroit Rivers and passes water into Lake Ontario by way of the Niagara River. Lake Ontario lies 326 feet below Lake Erie, and between the two lakes the waters of the Niagara drop over the world-famous Niagara Falls. French explorers, the first Europeans to reach the region, called Lake Erie *Lac Du Chat* (Lake of the Cat) for the Erieehronons, a tribe of Iroquois Indians that lived nearby whose name translated into "the people of the panther."

Pennsylvania Highway 5 follows the state's only true coastline, passing from near the Ohio state line at the southwest shore to the New York state line at the northeast shore, and offers regular vistas of the lake. To make the full Ohio-to–New York run, the traveler must begin on West Lake Road at the Ohio border and proceed east for a mile or so until it becomes Highway 5.

The highway is part of the Lake Erie Circle Tour, an auto route of about seven hundred miles through the states that have Lake Erie frontage. The Lake Erie Circle Tour is in turn part of the sixty-five-hundred-mile Great Lakes Circle Tour that connects all eight states and two Canadian provinces bordering the lakes. Both circle tours were created in the late 1980s and early 1990s by the Great Lakes Commission. Usually

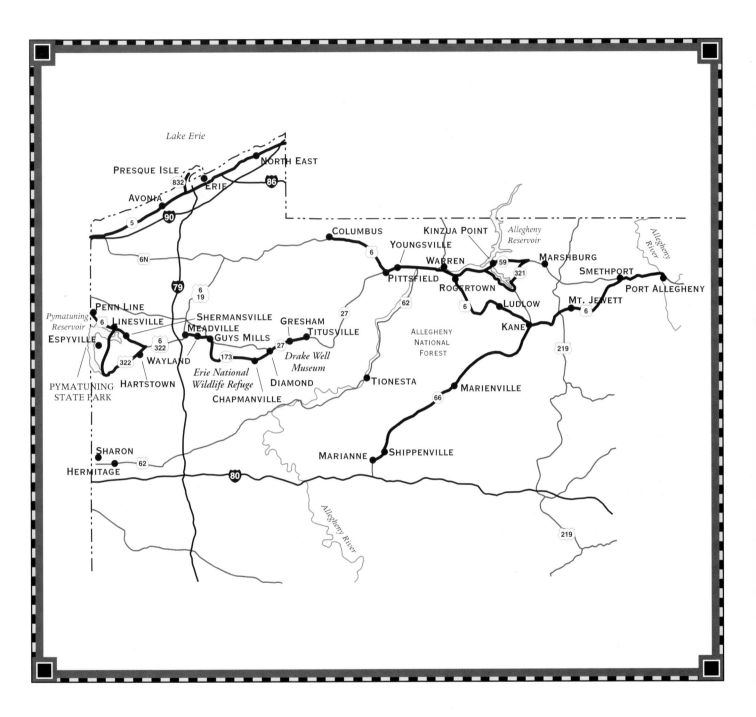

This colorful hot-air balloon provides a bird's-eye view of Pennsylvania's wonders below.

A fisherman's boat docks at the Manning access area of Pymatuning Lake in Crawford County.

A Blanding's turtle peers out of aquatic vegetation in a marsh on the shore of Lake Erie. Blanding's turtles are a threatened species in Pennsylvania.

Sand dunes stretch out along the coast of Lake Erie at Presque Isle.

following the major road or highway that is closest to the water, the tour routes are marked by distinctive green and white signs.

Highway 5 is also Pennsylvania's extension of the 454-mile Seaway Trail, a National Scenic Byway first established in New York State, and in a few places carries Bicycle Pennsylvania Route Z along its shoulders.

A flat, open coastal plain dominates the area surrounding the Great Lake, just as the words *lake, shore, Erie, bay, coast,* and *lakeside* dominate business and street names, and the nautical look of ocean resort homes dominates much of the region's residential architecture.

The area is highly developed, but a few spots like Springfield Township's Raccoon Park and the Pennsylvania Fish and Boat Commission's Elk Creek Access Area offer glimpses of the forested lakeside that once greeted the first humans to set foot here. Both natural areas lie just off Highway 5, the park at the bottom of a heavily wooded valley that runs from the highway to the lake, the access area along one of the most meandering streams in the entire state of Pennsylvania.

For some of our trip, Highway 5 stretches the definition of a backroad to the breaking point, as it approaches the city of Erie through an increasingly urbanized landscape. About midway through the city's strip of commercialization, however, our route intersects with Pennsylvania Highway 832 to lead the traveler to one of Pennsylvania's most fabled and visited natural sites—Presque Isle, a thirty-two-hundred-acre sandy peninsula that arches from the mainland out into Lake Erie. A national natural landmark, the peninsula is home to a greater number of Pennsylvania's endangered, threatened, and rare plant and animal species than any other site of comparable size in the state. It's also a premier stopover location for birds on their spring and summer migrations.

A few miles northeast of its intersection with Highway 832, our tour takes us through the city of Erie's manmade landscape of massive, old manufacturing plants, many of which now sit empty and rusting. It's a glimpse both at the former heyday of the district, when those plants were manned by thousands of workers, and the impact of the changing economic climate on a city of heavy industry.

Both southwest and northeast of Erie, the Pennsylvania Wine Country holds sway. Vineyards stretch out to Lake Erie on the northwest side of Highway 5 and seemingly to the horizon at some spots on the southeast. Although other parts of the state have been growing in this respect, most of Pennsylvania's four hundred grape farmers are located on this four-mile-wide coastal plain.

The Presque Isle lighthouse, illustrated in this 1940s postcard, was built in 1872.

11—PRESQUE ISLE LIGHT HOUSE, 1872, ERIE, PA.

4A-H2200

Since the early 1800s, the rich, quick-draining soils and proximity to the lake, which tends to temper harsh winter freezes, have drawn grape growers to this area of Pennsylvania and neighboring regions of New York and Ohio. The town of North East was home to the region's first winery, the former South Shore Wine Cellar, established in 1863 by William Griffith. The migration to the region was greatly speeded in the middle of the nineteenth century by the completion of the Erie Canal. Thus, wineries—with their ample taste-testing opportunities—abound along our route.

PENNSYLVANIA'S BIG SKY TOUR
THE PYMATUNING RESERVOIR

Although I've never heard it called such, I always think of the route we're about to follow around the Pymatuning Reservoir in Crawford County as Pennsylvania's Big Sky Tour. The incredibly flat landscape sprouts no mountains to get in the way of the sky, which seems to go on and on overhead. Vistas of wetlands abound from every slight rise of the terrain in this region, complete with wonderful bird-watching opportunities in the varied, wild habitat.

Begin in Penn Line at the Pennsylvania-Ohio border and travel southeast along U.S. Highway 6 to Linesville. The town was named for Amos Line, who in 1818 surveyed the area for the Pennsylvania Population Company. He then acquired land and built a mill on what is now Linesville Creek, upstream of the marsh that today is the bottom of Pymatuning Reservoir.

Even before Line's settlement of the site, the area around today's Pymatuning Reservoir was an important resource. Native Americans harvested salt, a valuable trading commodity, from the swamp that occupied the site until the 1930s. In the early 1900s, also before the creation of the reservoir, the swamp muck was used by local residents to grow large quantities of onions, which were shipped by rail to cities throughout Pennsylvania.

The reservoir, dammed in the early 1930s, served as flood control for the Shenango River and held the water supply for steel mills in the Shenango Valley. It eventually became a popular area for recreational tourism as well.

Not long after the construction of the dam near Linesville, locals noticed that carp gathered at the spillway to forage in the collection of flotsam that built up there. Someone tossed a crust of bread to the hungry fish, which erupted into a roiling mass. As the practice grew, wild ducks were also attracted to the free handouts. The frenzy of carp jockeying for bread was so tightly packed together that the waterfowl were able to stand atop them. Thus, the town was dubbed "Where the Ducks Walk on the Fish."

Word of the extraordinary sight soon spread beyond the local community, and stands selling stale bread for tourists to feed the fish and

THE ROUTE

Starting in Penn Line (Pennline), drive southeast on U.S. Highway 6 to Shermansville, take Shermansville Road south and U.S. Highway 322 southwest to Marshall Corners. Continue southwest on State Route 3008, then follow State Route 3005 north to Pymatuning State Park. Take Fries Road east to State Route 3011, and that route into Linesville.

Anglers enjoy the sunset at the Espyville marina on Pymatuning Lake.

ducks sprang up along the road out to the spillway. The attraction continues to support a snack bar and souvenir stand, where stacks of crates full of stale bread loaves are still delivered every day. Vehicles in the parking lot sport license plates from many different states.

The road from Linesville to the spillway is also home to the Pennsylvania Game Commission's Pymatuning Wildlife Learning Center. The center features a small but well-stocked museum of local birdlife, a nostalgic hunting heritage room, an abundance of hands-on activities for children, nature trails, and displays of wildlife habitat ideas for the home landscape. The large grassy knoll at the rear of the center provides a great overlook of the reservoir.

Nearby, the Pennsylvania Fish & Boat Commission's Linesville Fish Culture Station, where the agency raises various fish species for stocking Pennsylvania waters, offers visitors a view of a two-story, ten-thousand-gallon aquarium, filled with fish.

East of Linesville, just before the village of Shermansville, Highway 6 passes over the remains of the Erie Extension Canal, which ran 105 miles from New Castle to Erie, carrying barges from 1844 until 1871. More of the canal bed can be seen from the Highway 322 bridge just east of Hartstown, which is also home to the Hartstown Level Golf Course, one of the flattest courses in Pennsylvania.

IN THE MIDST OF OIL COUNTRY
ERIE NATIONAL WILDLIFE REFUGE

THE ROUTE

Drive west on Pennsylvania Highway 27 from Titusville. At Black Ash Corners take Varnell Road south to Johnson Road and follow that southwest to Sugar Lake Road, which runs northwest to Pennsylvania Highway 173. Drive north on Highway 173 to Pennsylvania Highway 27, then jog east to McFaden Road. Follow that north to Pennsylvania Highway 198, motor west to State Route 2013 at Guys Mills, then south to Shaffer Road, and west to New Road. Continue west on State Route 2032 to Wayland, then follow Highway 27 west to Meadville.

You will want to bring binoculars, drive very slowly, and make frequent stops on our next tour. Erie National Wildlife Refuge is a wildlife watcher's mecca.

The National Audubon Society has designated the refuge an Important Bird Area, as a total of 237 species of birds have been identified on the nearly nine thousand acres of the refuge. Waterfowl, such as hooded mergansers and blue-winged teal, are common resident nesting species. Bald eagles nest here, and rookeries of blue herons can also be found.

Nearly four dozen species of mammals live within the Erie National Wildlife Refuge's three distinct habitats: forest, field, and wetland. Beaver and muskrat are common sights in and near the ample waters. Deer, raccoons, rabbits, and other animals also populate the area in great numbers. You won't spot many of them from the road, or even from the many trails that slice through the wetlands, but at least thirty-seven species of reptiles and amphibians and dozens of species of native fish also share the refuge. And a wide variety of wildflowers—with the accompanying diversity of insect life, such as butterflies—can be viewed along all the trails and roadways as well.

Established in 1959, Erie National Wildlife Refuge lies thirty-five miles south of the city and lake of the same name. One of more than five hundred national wildlife refuges across the country, Erie consists of two separate divisions. The smaller and wilder Seneca Division encompasses the forested valleys around Muddy Creek and Dead Creek, southeast of Cambridge Springs. The more closely managed Sugar Lake Division, an area of spreading wetlands, beaver ponds, pools, and creeks near the village of Guys Mills, will be our focus.

Ironically, most of Sugar Lake, which the division is named for, lies outside the refuge and is largely a private recreation area. The lake, and its many private-property signs, is visible from Sugar Lake Road, which runs along its southwest side.

Our tour begins a bit to the east in Titusville, home of the oil industry and the annual Oil Festival and Parade. Founded in 1796 by Jonathan Titus and Samuel Kerr, Titusville is a typical northwestern Pennsylvania town. It has an architecturally interesting historic district, a soothing community park with a large gazebo and fountains in the center of town, and a considerably large stock of now-unused manufacturing plants.

Moving west on Pennsylvania Highway 27, through the last foothills we'll see before meeting the coastal plain that dominates the landscape around Lake Erie, we witness the many ways humans employ the earth's natural resources. West of Gresham, enormous horse farms stretch out into the distance. In and around the village of Diamond, gas wellheads sprout from front lawns and forest openings alike. Farmers work their fields of corn and grain. Near Chapmanville, a sand and gravel operation claws its aggregate products from the soil.

This is also one of Pennsylvania's Amish areas. The Amish are a religious group spread across twenty-two U.S. states and Ontario, Canada. As part of their beliefs, the Amish shun modern conveniences, such as electricity and motor vehicles. Signs warn the motorized traveler that he or she must share the road with and be cautious of the slower-moving horse-and-buggy rigs of the Plain People. One of their familiar one-room schoolhouses stands along McFadden Road, east of Mount Hope.

Areas of Meadville, the terminus for this tour, have a historic charm. Some streets in the village are still paved in red brick, and several fascinating collections wait to be discovered. The Baldwin-Reynolds House, former home of Supreme Court Justice Henry Baldwin, features household accoutrements from the mid 1800s, and a typical nineteenth century doctor's office is located next door. Pelletier Library on the campus of Allegheny College, which in 1815 was one of the first colleges founded west of the Allegheny Mountains, houses an array of Lincoln memorabilia. And the Johnson-Shaw Stereoscopic Museum collects, preserves, and exhibits stereoscopic products. Stereoscopes were optical instruments, all the rage in the early twentieth century, that converted two pictures taken of the same object from slightly different positions into a 3-D image. Keystone View Company, which operated in Meadville from 1892 to 1976, was at one time the largest stereoscopic photo company in the world.

RIGHT:

The carp are so concentrated at the spillway on Pymatuning Lake, that at times ducks can literally walk on the fish. Here, Darlene Davis throws bread to the carp. Visitors can purchase stale bread from a vendor that may sell several thousand loaves a day during the summer tourist season.

BELOW LEFT:

The Drake Well Museum at Titusville offers many insights into the history of Pennsylvania's oil industry. It was at this spot that the world's first successful oil well operated. Locomotives once regularly stopped at the train platform pictured here to transport barrels of black gold far and wide.

BELOW RIGHT:

A sign at Linesville welcomes visitors.

A nest of baby cottontails blends into nature's surroundings. Rabbits are common residents of the Erie National Wildlife Refuge, as are beaver, muskrat, deer, raccoon, and many other wildlife species.

FIRST IN OIL: THE DRAKE WELL MUSEUM

Although visions of J. R. Ewing and the sprawling Southfork ranch of television's *Dallas* fame or the shadowy dealings of Enron come to mind for most of us when we hear the word "oil," the oil industry actually began in the swamps of northwestern Pennsylvania. On August 27, 1859, at what is today Titusville, Edwin Drake hit pay dirt with the world's first oil well.

The 219-acre Drake Well Museum marks the spot of that first strike with operating reproductions of Drake's steam engine and wood-fired boiler; more than eighty exhibits about the origin of oil and the oil industry; ten thousand early photographs of the oil region during the boom era; and a twenty-eight-minute film featuring Vincent Price as Edwin Drake.

Drake, an agent for the Seneca Oil Company of New Haven, Connecticut, didn't discover oil. Petroleum has been known and used for thousands of years. However, demand for crude skyrocketed in the late 1850s, when various inventors developed procedures to refine it into kerosene. The supply available by collecting the crude from surface seeps just wasn't enough to meet that new demand. Drake was sent into the wilds of northwestern Pennsylvania to find a way to boost production, which he did by adapting the drilling technique that others were using to excavate salt water. At just sixty-nine feet, he struck a source of oil that would produce twenty barrels per day, which was double the rate of production of any other contemporary source.

His work paved the way for an oil boom in the region. Derricks and pumps of speculators soon filled the landscape along Oil Creek. The resulting oil glut drove prices down so far that Drake and his partners left the business by 1862.

"Torpedoing a Well near Titusville, Pa." reads this vintage postcard.

LONGHOUSE SCENIC DRIVE
THE ALLEGHENY RESERVOIR AND
ALLEGHENY NATIONAL FOREST

Longhouse Scenic Drive, running along the Kinzua Bay portion of the Allegheny Reservoir in Warren and McKean Counties, is a both a trip through a wild and rugged place and a glimpse into our ability to chain the forces of nature. Steep, densely forested mountainsides that drop into the depths of the reservoir showcase nature's splendor. Kinzua Dam, a massive blockage of concrete and steel that backs up the mighty Allegheny River into the reservoir, is the primary evidence of human impact. The thunderous roar of the outflow from the dam—roll down your windows; you can hear it at a great distance—is a sign, however, that nature's power still remains in that water.

Completed in 1965, the Kinzua Dam flood-control facility rises 179 feet above the streambed to harness the Allegheny into a twelve-thousand-acre impoundment that stretches north into Seneca Indian lands in New York State's Cattaraugus County. It's part of the flood-control system operated by the U.S. Army Corps of Engineers for the Allegheny and Upper Ohio River basins.

The immense back-up of water also gave rise to the construction of a huge circular pond, sixty-six feet deep, a half-mile in diameter, and large enough to be included on topographic maps, just southeast of the dam. The hilltop pond is part of a pumped storage hydroelectric plant originally licensed in 1965 to the Pennsylvania Electric Company and the Cleveland Electric Illuminating Company but operated today by First Energy Corporation of Akron, Ohio. Supply and discharge tunnels twenty-two feet in diameter and a half-mile long connect the much-larger, primary reservoir to the hydropower plant and the power plant to the smaller, upper reservoir.

Equally impressive is nature's display in this remote area, from the rapids-packed Allegheny River as we begin our tour on Pennsylvania Highway 59 in Rogertown to the mountainside overlooks and vistas throughout the entire trip.

A profitable first stop is the Kinzua Point Information Center, off Highway 59 at the dam. Displays inside tell the story of the dam and reservoir, and brochures and maps on nearly every aspect of the area are available as well.

Our route runs primarily along Forest Road 262, which presents several fantastic views without asking us to even leave our vehicles, and also offers several side trips for additional panoramas of the reservoir and wild landscape. Big Bend Overlook, and Jakes Rocks Overlook and Picnic Area, are the first of many potential side trips. Rimrock Overlook can be found near the end of our tour, before Highway 59 crosses the reservoir on Cornplanter Bridge.

THE ROUTE

From Rogertown, go east on Pennsylvania Highway 59 to Forest Road 262. Drive southeast, then turn north on Pennsylvania Highway 321. Follow Highway 321 to Pennsylvania Highway 59, and follow that to Kinzua Point.

ABOVE:

A field of daisies springs up near the dam at Tionesta Lake off Highway 36 in Forest County.

RIGHT:

Irises, also known as blue flags, grow in the Allegheny National Forest.

ABOVE LEFT:
Pink foxgloves are a vivid example of northwestern Pennsylvania's various wildflowers.

ABOVE RIGHT:
This male bluebird is one of the many species that birders can look for in Pennsylvania's natural areas.

LEFT:
Showy lady's slipper orchids can be found in Erie County in late June.

ALLEGHENY NATIONAL FOREST

Straddling the Allegheny Plateau, the Allegheny National Forest encompasses 513,257 acres in Elk, Forest, McKean, and Warren Counties. Designated a national forest by President Calvin Coolidge in 1923, the ANF is Pennsylvania's only national forest and one of 155 nationwide.

It offers something for every outdoor interest. Crisscrossing the huge tracts of forest are more than seven hundred miles of trails, ranging from strolls of less than a mile to the eighty-seven-mile leg of the extended-stay North Country Trail that cuts through the forest. About 115 miles of trails have been designated for snowmobile use. A total of nineteen campgrounds are spread throughout the ANF, including seven that are boat- or hiking-access only. Water enthusiasts of all kinds find accommodations for their pursuits on bodies ranging from the massive Allegheny Reservoir to the Allegheny and Clarion Rivers to a myriad of smaller streams.

Included in Pennsylvania's lone national forest are the state's only federally designated wilderness areas: the 8,663-acre Hickory Creek Wilderness, south of Warren, and the seven-island, 368-acre Allegheny River Islands Wilderness, near Tionesta. Designated a national wilderness in 1984, but formed of sand and clay deposits centuries earlier, the islands are characterized by river-bottom habitats dominated by maple and sycamore trees. The largest is 96-acre Crull's Island, followed by Thompson's, 67 acres; Baker, 67 acres; Courson, 62 acres; King, 36 acres; R. Thompson's, 30 acres; and No-Name, 10 acres. There are no developed trails on any of the islands, but they are open for public exploration and overnight camping.

Allegheny National Forest, which surrounds Kinzua, is full of opportunities for recreation, ranging from swimming and picnicking to fishing and boating to camping and extended backpacking. Any outdoor taste or comfort level can be accommodated. The Dewdrop Recreation Area on Kinzua Bay, for example, offers many of the amenities of home: It has seventy-four family campsites—each with a picnic table, fire ring, and tent pad—flush toilets, hot showers, a children's play area, a beach, and a concrete boat launch.

Illustrating the other extreme is the more rugged North Country Trail, which we cross just before turning onto Pennsylvania Highway 321 for the second half of our tour. A National Scenic Trail, the North Country Trail links natural, recreational, historic, and cultural points in seven northern states: Michigan, Minnesota, New York, North Dakota, Ohio, Pennsylvania, and Wisconsin. When completed it will extend forty-four-hundred miles from Crown Point in New York to Lake Sakakawea State Park on the Missouri River in North Dakota. The Pennsylvania portion, which is about 180 miles long and halfway completed, crosses McKean, Forest, and Warren Counties.

THE FOREST FOR THE TREES
ROUTE 66

In good times and in bad, for better or for worse, trees and forestry dominate the region we'll pass through on this tour. A significant part of the area's workforce is connected to the wood product industry, whether in logging operations, wood product manufacturing, or the service industry supported by income from forestry. Local controversy, such as debates over how much and what type of logging should be allowed or the impact of off-road vehicles on the forest ecosystem, revolves around the region's top resource. Much of the Allegheny National Forest shows the scars of the logging industry, but signs of more modern, environmentally friendly operations are visible as well, as they bring the next generation of trees to maturity.

It's not difficult to find forest-related industry in Kane, at the beginning of our route. Kane Hardwoods, launched in 1855, is the largest private landowner in Pennsylvania, with 126,000 acres in its various tracts throughout the region. Holgate Toy Company, just off Poplar Street, has been manufacturing an incredible variety of wooden toys, such as train sets, cars, blocks, and yo-yos, since 1929. The company operates a small museum and store outlet, which has a public window into its factory.

Kane also proudly bills itself as the black cherry capital of the world and celebrates a three-day black cherry festival each July. It's a justified claim, as fully 80 percent of the world's valuable cherry hardwood originates in this region.

General Thomas L. Kane, the first Pennsylvanian to volunteer to fight in the Civil War and organizer of the glory-covered Bucktail Regiment, founded Kane in 1865. He called it Clarion Summit for the Clarion River, which originates nearby, but his fame led residents to change the name to Kane Summit, which was eventually shortened to Kane. The Thomas L. Kane Memorial Chapel and Museum, owned by the Church of Jesus Christ of Latter-Day Saints, houses Kane family heirlooms, including a tea set once used by Thomas Jefferson. Other memorabilia and relics of the Kane family can be found at the circa-1897 Kane Manor Country Inn, today a bed and breakfast but once the home of the Kane family after General Kane's death.

Allegheny National Forest, through which our winding and bending course along Route 66 cuts, bills itself as the "Land of Many Uses." The forest offers something for every outdoor interest, and hiking trails and all-terrain-vehicle/snowmobile trails intersect Route 66 at many spots. Just after we cross the North Country Trail, the forest gives us a taste of its dominance on the region's landscape. Even at midday there is a darkness under the tree canopy more attuned to dusk.

THE ROUTE

Follow Pennsylvania Highway 66 west from Kane to Marianne.

ABOVE:

Mail Pouch barns grace the edges of highways across the country. This example stands beside Pennsylvania Highway 36 near Cook Forest in Jefferson County.

FACING PAGE:

A picturesque byway winds through the flaming foliage of the Allegheny National Forest near Marshburg.

Marienville, which names itself as the snowmobile capital of Pennsylvania, has made the most of the growing demand for ATV and snowmobile travel in the state. Some of the town's streets also serve as designated snowmobile lanes during winter. And the Marienville Winterfest, usually held the last week of January, is one big celebration of travel over snow and ice, right down to the snowmobile torchlight parade.

When driving our section of Highway 66, from Kane in McKean County to Marianne in Clarion County, keep an eye out for barn signs. This route might be Pennsylvania's champion for the most barn walls still wearing Mail Pouch Tobacco advertisements painted on their siding. I counted a half-dozen of the pop-historical images that spout "Chew Mail Pouch Tobacco" and "Treat yourself to the best, Mail Pouch Tobacco."

Bloch Brothers Tobacco Company, originators of the Mail Pouch brand, launched the barn-sign idea at the turn of the twentieth century, offering to paint a farmer's barn for free and thereafter paying him five dollars per year or free tobacco products. Mail Pouch ads reached their peak in the 1930s and prospered as an advertising medium until 1965 when President Lyndon Johnson signed the Highway Beautification Act that restricted commercial signs close to highways. The Mail Pouch barn painting program ended in 1996, when the last barn painter, Harley Warrick of Belmont, Ohio, retired after fifty years and thirty thousand barns.

RIVER VALLEY ROUTE
EXPLORING ROUTE 6

THE ROUTE

Take U.S. Highway 6 west from Port Allegheny to Columbus.

Following Route 6 (U.S. Highway 6) through McKean and Warren Counties gives the traveler a small sense of what route-finding was like for the pioneers of the region, or even the explorers of the American West. As the highway snakes its way from one Pennsylvania town to the next, it follows river valleys and passes, with the Allegheny Mountains towering on both sides all the while. It made much more sense for the explorers and pioneers to travel with relative ease—emphasis on the word "relative"—along the river bottoms than across the mountainsides.

As U.S. 6 hooks west out of Port Allegheny, this valley route is evident: It follows Ostrander Hollow to Smethport; then Marvin Creek through Kasson and Hazel Hurst; Kane Creek into Mt. Jewett; mountain valleys through Kane and Westmore; Twomile Run northwesterly through Ludlow; the beginnings of Tionesta Creek through Roystone into Sheffield; the West Branch of the Tionesta to Rogerstown and Warren; the Allegheny River to Irvine; Brokenstraw Creek through Youngsville to Pittsfield; Little Brokenstraw Creek into Freehold; and, finally, an overland route into Columbus. If you want even more of a sense of how the pioneers pushed along such routes, just jump out of your car, put on thirty pounds of gear, and trek along the bank of one of these streams.

National Geographic magazine named Route 6, which stretches from the Atlantic to the Pacific, one America's most scenic drives. The portion of the national roadway that runs through McKean and Warren Counties is certainly among the most beautiful areas of the entire route.

Some have also dubbed Route 6 the Victorian Region of northwestern Pennsylvania for the large numbers of stately brick and wooden homes and commercial buildings erected there in the 1800s by wealthy lumber or oil barons and shopkeepers. Festivals in many of the communities along Route 6 still pay tribute to the towns' glory days, when the lumber and oil industries were pumping steady streams of big money into the region. Mt. Jewett's Swedish Festival each fall is one example, recalling the heritage of the Swedish immigrants who found employment in the area as sawers or woodworkers.

Many of the original structures flanking Route 6, which serves as main street for several communities, have been maintained and refurbished—often whole blocks of them. Thus, the traveler can observe residential and commercial districts that look much today as they did a century ago.

Smethport, home to America's First Christmas Store, which started as a sideline in a drug store in 1935, might be the quaintest of these communities of yesteryear. The town is also home to the Allegheny Arms and Armor Museum, which houses a collection of heavy armaments used by American soldiers over the years, and the museum of the McKean County Historical Society, which holds artifacts dating to the 1700s.

Warren, on the other hand, has maintained the largest concentration of historic structures. More than six hundred buildings, of twenty-five different styles, have been cataloged in the Warren Historic District, which encompasses twenty-eight blocks in the heart of a city that offers twenty-one parks totaling 180 acres. Warren is also home to the headquarters of the Blair Corporation, a name which nearly all Sunday newspaper readers will recognize from its mail-order inserts that advertise jackets, pants, and the like. The company, originally founded in 1910 by John L. Blair Sr. as the New Process Rubber Company, is run out of a commanding building erected for the company in 1928 along Third Avenue.

To the west, the village of Pittsfield recalls a much different bit of local history: the Pittsfield Riot of July 1866. Men from the community and from the Great Fitzpatrick Circus, in town for a performance, drank and gambled together one night after the show. The festivities soon deteriorated into a battle with clubs and fists that lasted from midnight to morning. Noncombatants barred their doors, hid in sheds, and climbed trees to escape the melée.

The retelling of that incident shows us a darker side to local history as we travel past and marvel at the wondrous mansions from another age and imagine their stories. There is more than quaintness in the history here.

PART II

WILD AS IT COMES:
NORTH-CENTRAL PENNSYLVANIA

FACING PAGE:
Red and gold fall leaves surround a white birch log on the west rim of Pennsylvania's Grand Canyon, Pine Creek Gorge.

ABOVE:
Potter County is home to many views of rustic farmland.

The north-central region of Pennsylvania is a land of extremes—from the Penn State–centered prosperity of the Nittany Valley to the hard times of struggling villages, from large, rolling farms in the south to small patches carved out of the woodlands in the north, from natural wonders like the Pennsylvania Grand Canyon to manmade marvels like the almost never-ending Route 6.

Classic small-town business districts with local stores are found throughout the area, surviving—for the most part—under the protection of distance from large cities and the domination of retail chains. Heritage and history are essential to residents, and they've gone out of their way to both preserve and share through sites like the Pennsylvania Lumber Museum and the Mifflinburg Buggy Museum. Similarly, the sprawling campus of Penn State University seems to have museums tucked away in nearly every out-of-the-way corner, with collections ranging from art to cable television paraphernalia to insects.

It's a wild land, probably the wildest that Pennsylvania still has to offer. Deer outnumber people in many areas. Bear roam in ever-growing numbers. Elk populations, although fairly isolated and restricted in current range, are increasing and spreading into new peripheral areas. Throughout the region, prime wildlife viewing spots abound.

PENNSYLVANIA'S NORTHERN TIER
ROUTE 6 CONTINUES

THE ROUTE

From Burtville, take U.S. Highway 6 east to Mainesburg.

Route 6 (U.S. Highway 6) is Pennsylvania's longest highway, stretching more than four hundred miles from Milford at the New Jersey state line to Penn Line at the Ohio state line. It slices through eleven counties, following a route originally laid out to connect all the county seats of the state's northern tier.

Pennsylvania's Route 6 traces its origin to early Native American footpaths that led through virgin forests. Before the nineteenth century, much of what would become Route 6 existed as a series of trails leading to the Seneca nation to the north, in today's New York State. As European settlers moved westward, thriving lumber towns developed across the northern tier and a loose collection of roads and pathways soon connected those towns. Much of the roadway that would eventually be designated as Route 6 already existed by 1927, when the first signposts began to mark the new highway.

For a brief time in the early 1900s, Route 6 was known as the Theodore Roosevelt Highway, but the Sons of the Union Veterans of the Civil War successfully lobbied to rename it "The Grand Army of the Republic Highway" in 1937. The Grand Army of the Republic was an organization formed by veterans of the Civil War in an effort to continue the camaraderie of friendships forged in battle.

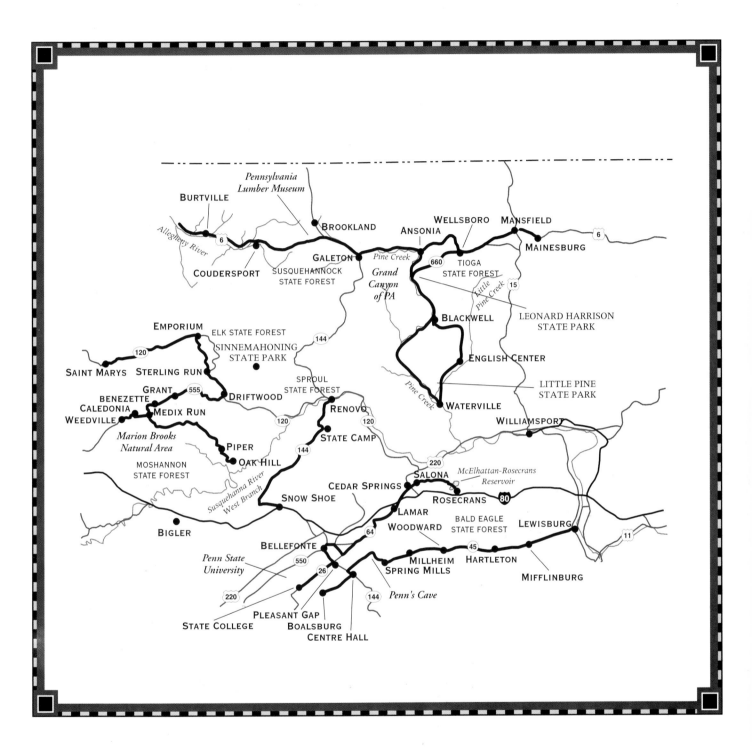

OVERLEAF:

Pennsylvania's longest highway, Route 6, offers this sweeping view of the Keystone State from Warrior's Path Overlook at Wyalusing in Bradford County.

THE PENNSYLVANIA LUMBER MUSEUM

The Pennsylvania Lumber Museum, midway between Coudersport and Galeton, preserves and interprets the tools, methods, and men of one of the most important eras in the northern tier's history.

From 1850 to 1870, the center of the lumber industry moved to northern and central Pennsylvania as timber stock dwindled farther south. Although Williamsport, with its strategic location on the Susquehanna River and twenty-nine operating sawmills, became known as the lumber capital of the world, the product itself was coming from the great forests of the northern tier. Town after town was born and developed as loggers strained to meet the demands of a growing nation. During that period, Pennsylvania was the greatest lumber-producing state in the country.

This postcard from 1911 depicts the Goodyear Mills and log basin at Galeton.

By 1920, the seemingly endless forests of Pennsylvania were gone. In hundreds of lumber towns, the sawmill whistle was given a final blast, which signaled the closing of the mill and the end of an era. Loggers moved to West Virginia and the Great Lakes states, leaving behind thousands of devastated, treeless acres.

The Pennsylvania Lumber Museum captures all of that history with a re-created logging camp—stocked with the actual equipment and necessities of the men who worked there—interpretive displays, and a two-day Bark Peeler's Convention held every July. Trying to remain faithful to the original summer gatherings among real lumber camp workers, the convention features competitions in lumberjack skills, as well as events like frog jumping, fiddling, and tobacco spitting, and a craft fair that shows the craftsmen plying their skills

Although several of the other routes in this book intersect with highlights along U.S. 6, for sheer representation of Pennsylvania's northern tier we've chosen just the Potter and Tioga sections of the roadway for this trip. Every town, river, and state park along the length of U.S. 6 has its own unique tale. But anyone who has driven along it from Burtville in western Potter County to Mainesburg in eastern Tioga County, with both eye and mind open, can truly claim a sense of the northern tier.

The traveler will cruise through unbroken stretches of the often dense Susquehannock State Forest, spotting the deer that munch roadside grasses at almost any time of the year and the hen turkeys that bring their broods there for the insects in late spring and summer. Although impressive, the forests of today's northern tier are lacking when compared to the virgin white pine and hemlock forest that covered this region until the mid-nineteenth century. So dense was that timber that little sunlight reached the forest floor, even on the brightest days, inspiring the name "Black Forest."

Explorers of Route 6 will encounter the wild rivers and streams that have carved their way into the Allegheny Mountains—the upper Allegheny River, the West Branch, and Pine Creek. In a farmer's field on a hillside just north of Brookland is a rainwater runoff spot that can claim to be the starting point for the Allegheny River, which flows west to Pittsburgh; the Susquehanna River, which slices south through the middle of Pennsylvania to eventually empty into the Chesapeake Bay; and the Genesee River, which flows north into New York.

U.S. 6 travelers will also shop, dine, and tour the quintessential northern-tier, commercial-hub towns of Coudersport and Wellsboro, with their active and diverse business districts. Downtown Coudersport remains such an excellent example of a nineteenth-century small town that it's been named to the National Register of Historic Places. Wellsboro, which is covered in more detail in the next section, exhibits the same Victorian styling. The Tioga County Courthouse in Wellsboro, with its circa-1832 Greek Ionic columns, is the oldest courthouse in the state still used for its original purpose. The rustic, everyday history of the region is also preserved and displayed in places like the Pennsylvania Lumber Museum near Walton and the Tioga County Historical Society Museum in Wellsboro.

THE GRAND CANYON OF PENNSYLVANIA
PINE CREEK GORGE

Known as the Grand Canyon of Pennsylvania to tourists and the Pine Creek Gorge to locals, the forty-seven-mile-long cut into the mountains of Tioga State Forest—a thousand feet deep and four thousand feet from rim to rim at its most sensational—is the most awe-inspiring natural wonder in the state.

From any of the abundant vistas along the rims of the canyon, onlookers seem to stand atop the world, with a panorama of dense Pennsylvania forest spreading out below and before them. The view is broken only sporadically by landscape features like Pine Creek, rendered toylike by the sheer distance to its course on the canyon floor.

Official descriptions give the canyon a length of forty-seven miles, from Ansonia in the north to Waterville in the south. But the truly breathtaking part of the canyon, with its sharply rising walls, exists in only the northernmost twenty miles, from just south of Ansonia in the north to Blackwell in the south.

Until about twenty thousand years ago, the headwaters of Pine Creek flowed northeasterly from Ansonia. Then continental glaciers covered the area, eventually melting and retreating, and dropping debris that dammed the normal flow of water. That forced the creek to flow south, and the abundant melting waters of the glacier swiftly carved the deep canyon and today's water course.

THE ROUTE

From Blackwell, take West Rim Road north; make a right onto Painter Letonia Road and drive north; make another right onto Colton Road and follow it north to U.S. Highway 6. Drive east on U.S. 6 into Wellsboro, then follow Pennsylvania Highway 660 west to Leonard Harrison State Park.

Horse-drawn sleighs provide rides all day long at Wellsboro's winter festival.

This log hauler and lifter, featured at the Pennsylvania Lumber Museum, was used to move logs at lumber camps in Potter County.

At the Pennsylvania Lumber Museum, on Route 6 between Coudersport and Galeton, travelers can explore the state's logging history.

ABOVE:

Pine Creek runs through the Grand Canyon of Pennsylvania, a mighty gorge that stretches fifty miles and plunges a thousand feet deep. The canyon is one of the most magnificent natural wonders in the state.

LEFT:

The Austin Dam, built in 1909 by the Bayless Pulp and Paper Company to supply water to their paper mill, is located southwest of Coudersport on Highway 872. "The dam that could not break" failed on September 30, 1911, and destroyed the town of Austin.

For the motoring traveler, the dramatic rise from the floor of the canyon to the lofty heights of the rim is best experienced soon after our route leaves Blackwell, turns right onto the gravel-covered West Rim Road, and follows that road north through Tioga State Forest. Vistas on the rim of the canyon offer the best view, but as West Rim Road becomes steeper and steeper to climb, the true sense of the canyon's depth is most acutely felt. As my eight-year-old son, Casey, exaggerated slightly, "It's straight up!"

As West Rim Road nears the rim of the canyon, rustic overlooks with ample parking become regular and nicely spaced for stopping to see the surrounding area. The most developed overlook—and the one most heavily utilized by tourists—is on the east rim at Leonard Harrison State Park, but those on the west rim offer much more diverse views out over and down into the canyon. They're also generally less crowded.

From each of the lookouts, after the far-flung grandeur of the overall scene is absorbed, the most instantly noticed landscape feature is the northernmost twenty miles of the Pine Creek Rail Trail, a crushed limestone bike path alongside Pine Creek on the canyon's floor. The trail, which *USA Today* rated as one of the "10 Great Places" in the world for a bike tour, is covered further in the Little Pine Creek Region tour, our next trip.

Each side of the canyon has its own state park. The Civilian Conservation Corps developed 368-acre Colton Point State Park on the west rim from 1933 to 1936. Named for Henry Colton, a local lumberman, in 1988 the park became a National Historic Landmark Park in tribute to the CCC era. On the opposite rim sits 585-acre Leonard Harrison State Park. It is named for the civic-minded Wellsboro businessman and banker who owned and developed the original 121-acre site, around what was then known as "The Lookout," and then gave it to the state of Pennsylvania in 1922.

Driving toward Leonard Harrison State Park along Pennsylvania Highway 660, south from Wellsboro, the visitor passes Animaland Zoological Park, which since 1954 has been a favorite with the younger set. The nicely shaded park showcases a wide variety of animals from around the world and offers special features, like a bridge over a pond packed with dozens of hungry bullhead catfish, regular public feedings of the giraffe, and a heavily populated petting zoo.

Most of the towns along this route are tiny hamlets, offering little to pause the traveler. Wellsboro is the notable exception. A typical commercial hub of Pennsylvania's northern tier, further bolstered by strong tourist traffic through most of the year, Wellsboro offers a thriving and diverse business district of varied restaurants, stores, and specialty shops. Several neighborhoods feature nicely maintained and restored Victorian architecture, notably Pearl Street, which has an overall nineteenth-century feel.

TRAILS AND TOWNS
THE LITTLE PINE CREEK REGION

Some of the wildest country in Pennsylvania swallows travelers soon after they leave the village of Waterville, commercial hub for the area, to begin the journey north on State Route 4001. The thick forest of towering Huntley Mountain presses from the left, while Little Pine Creek twists and turns along its rocky course on the right. Bear, deer, bobcat, turkey, porcupine, and many other critters are likely to be spotted at any point along the drive.

Classic Pennsylvania hunting camps and lodges perch here and there, remnants of those days when the lure of big-game hunting drew hordes of sportsmen from southern parts of the state for week-long stays in November and December.

Little Pine State Park, which began as Civilian Conservation Corps Camp S-129 in 1933 and became a public campground in 1958, is the first major break in the forest. One of the most unusual features of the park is a collection of aged grave markers on a small knoll among the campsites. It's the cemetery of the former village of English Mills, founded in 1816 to accommodate the families of loggers. The village was formed around two sawmills operated by John and James English, who in 1782 were the first American settlers in the Little Pine Valley.

Little Pine Creek is one of the hundreds of smaller streams that fed logs by the millions into Williamsport, which at one time was home to more millionaires than any other U.S. city. The last raft of logs moved down the Little Pine in 1909.

With fourteen miles of trails within the park, Little Pine State Park is a hiker's dream. From the family-oriented, wildflower-lined, mile-long Carsontown Trail to the scenic but difficult Panther Run Trail, every level of ability and skill can be matched. The five-mile Lake Shore Trail, which runs along the eastern, non-developed side of the ninety-four-acre Little Pine Lake, is a truly wild and remote experience.

A bit farther north, Carsontown is a tiny collection of homes and hunting camps. Wildlife feeders at the rear of many of the camps regularly attract black bears for early evening dinners, providing fantastic viewing. The Community Church in town turned one hundred in 2001, but is a mere babe in comparison to the Shawnee village and cemetery believed to have occupied the spot centuries before, when the Iroquoian and Algonquian peoples used the area as a hunting ground.

THE ROUTE

From Waterville, follow State Route 4001 north to the village of English Center, follow Pennsylvania Highway 287 north to State Route 4002, make a left onto State Route 4002, and follow it through the village of Oregon Hill. Turn right onto Township Road 442 (which eventually becomes Big Run Road) and follow it into the village of Blackwell. Turn left onto Pennsylvania Highway 414 and follow it west then south back to Waterville.

This historical image of a street scene in downtown Williamsport was shot in the early twentieth century.

Little Pine Creek was once used to transport logs to Williamsport, which became known as the lumber capital of the world. Today, anglers and boaters are more common sights along the creek.

Trout lilies and other early spring wildflowers abound in many of Pennsylvania's natural areas.

The Keystone State has healthy populations of many native wildlife species, including beaver, which are spreading across the state in increasing numbers.

North of Carsontown, the village of English Center lies across a metal suspension bridge that was added to the National Register of Historic Places in 1978. Built in 1891 by Dean & Westbrook of New York, the three-hundred-foot-long bridge carries the traveler over Little Pine Creek for a look at several homes constructed of native river rock. This is the area where the colony known as the "English Settlement" was founded in the early 1800s by the Reverend John Hey of the Independent Church of England, based in Philadelphia, and a band of settlers he lured from Haven Parish in England. Unprepared for the rigors of clearing home sites from mature forests and surviving harsh winter conditions with meager rations, the emigrants soon became disillusioned and began abandoning the colony. Enoch Blackwell and his son, William, left their clearing at what is today Oregon Hill in 1811 and moved to a spot at the southern extremity of the Pennsylvania Grand Canyon, now known as the village of Blackwell.

The Mid-State Trail, a 261-mile hiking trail that runs from the Mason-Dixon Line in south-central Pennsylvania to Blackwell, crosses our route just before we emerge from the dense forest into the village. Blackwell also offers an access point for the Pine Creek Rail Trail, which extends twenty miles from Waterville north into the canyon. The trail was built atop the bed of what was once the Jersey Shore, Pine Creek & Buffalo Railroad, which began carrying timber to sawmills in 1883.

A fitting conclusion, on our return to Waterville, is a visit to the Waterville Country Store, which for decades has offered groceries, camping needs, sporting goods, and tourist trinkets. It also offers a taste of the vanishing all-purpose stores that once inhabited every hamlet and crossroads in the region.

BUGLING GIANTS
PENNSYLVANIA'S ELK RANGE

THE ROUTE

Take Pennsylvania Highway 555 east from Weedville to Township Road 424 and follow that north and east to Grant Hill Road. Drive southeast to Grant, then motor east on Highway 555 to Driftwood. Take Pennsylvania Highway 120 north to Sterling Run, Township Road 308 northwest to May Hollow Road, May Hollow Road northwest to State Route 3001, State Route 3001 north to Emporium, and Highway 120 west to Saint Marys.

Drive this route slowly with every eye in your vehicle scanning the woodlands and scattered fields alongside the road. (Well, the driver might want to keep his or her eyes on the road.) At any point during the trip, particularly in the late afternoon through early morning hours, one or more five-hundred-pound representatives of Pennsylvania's growing elk herd might appear.

This is elk country Pennsylvania style. An estimated eight hundred of the big animals roam this region, mostly within a few miles of the route we're driving. Approximately sixty thousand tourists cram this region each year, mostly from late August into early October, to get a look at the elk. Unless the annual Elk Expo, held in late September, is central to your plans, a trip outside the tourism peak is highly recommended. The elk populate the area year-round, although they are more concentrated and easier to locate during the breeding season.

Until quite recently, remarkably few tourist attractions had grown around the elk herd. The Benezette Store in the town of the same name

Eastern Elk once ranged across Pennsylvania, but colonization and exploitation by European settlers quickly set the species on a downward spiral. By the 1850s, wild elk still roamed only Cameron, Elk, and McKean Counties, and, by the late 1870s, the species had been extirpated from the state.

In 1913, however, the Pennsylvania Game Commission began redevelopment of the elk population, first with a single-minded stocking of fifty western elk from Yellowstone National Park. Their efforts continued in fits and spurts, with several long periods of neglect, but the commission eventually created a solid pioneering program of habitat development, elk research, and elk relocation.

The results are a herd estimated at eight hundred in 2002 and projected to reach nearly thirteen hundred by 2005.

---

has perennially offered a few photos, emblazoned caps, shirts, and vehicle plates. Shops like the Elk Country Craft and Gift Shop in Medix Run are starting to offer a variety of higher quality regional items, many related to the elk. A few books and videos about the herd are also beginning to turn up in local convenience stores. The preferred method to see the elk, however, is simply to drive along the route described here and look for the massive-antlered elk strolling through backyards and along the road.

Just off Pennsylvania Highway 555, a couple miles west of Driftwood, the former village of Mix Run contains one of the region's few attractions not related to the elk herd. The Tom Mix Birthplace Park, missed by most tourists because of the very small signs marking its location, is the site of the former logging community where actor Tom Mix was born. The creation and passion of Ray and Eva Flaugh, the park houses an extensive collection of paraphernalia from the movie and radio career of the "King of the Cowboys."

Also deserving of attention is Saint Marys, a quickly developing commercial hub for the region. Most major restaurant chains have joined the town's eatery scene, which already offered a variety of local establishments worth a visit. Chain retail stores have also set up shop here, although the downtown business district continues to thrive.

THE QUEHANNA WILDERNESS AREA
MEDIX RUN TO OAK HILL

Driving the Quehanna Highway is a singular experience. There's almost no traffic along this only paved road through the Quehanna Wilderness Area of the Moshannon State Forest.

A few hunting and fishing camps in the villages of Medix Run and Oak Hill, a gas company's pumping station, and, between the two villages, a 1950s nuclear engine testing facility now used as a prison boot camp are the only significant imprints man has made on this naturescape.

Tom Mix, a native of Pennsylvania, starred in numerous silent Western films from 1909 through 1935.

THE ROUTE

From Medix Run, drive south and southeast on the Quehanna Highway (this begins as State Route 2004 and later, after crossing the Cameron-Clearfield county line, becomes State Route 1011). South of Piper, motor east on Township Road 111 into Oak Hill.

TOP:

A striking view of Sinnemahoning Creek can be seen from the Driftwood bridge in Cameron County. Sinnemahoning State Park is located on the first fork of the creek.

ABOVE:

This majestic bull elk, seen near Benezette, is a fine example of the state's growing elk herd.

A woodcarver brings a bear to life at the annual Ridgway Chainsaw Carvers Rendezvous in Elk County. The event attracts carvers from all over the world.

The Quehanna Wilderness Area features the Marion Brooks Natural Area, which has acres of beautiful white birch trees.

The former nuclear engine facility was developed and operated by the Curtiss-Wright Company on fifty thousand acres sold to the company by the state in 1955 at a point on the map designated as Piper. The site, along with clean-up responsibilities for the nuclear waste and contaminated facilities, was returned to the state in 1966. While clean-up continues at some parts of the complex, in 1992 other parts were converted into the Pennsylvania Department of Correction's Quehanna Motivational Boot Camp. Minimum-security inmates assigned to the camp undergo a rigid six-month disciplinary and training program, which, if successfully completed, results in their immediate release on parole.

As interesting as the area's varied history may be, nature is the true star of the Quehanna Highway. Medix Run, and the side of the mountain at the beginning of this tour, are prime elk-viewing spots. The "elk crossing" signs mean business. Bear, turkey, deer, and coyote are seen regularly along the entire route.

The star of stars on this trip is the 975-acre Marion Brooks Natural Area, the state's largest stand of white birch, which is located in the middle of the tour. The stand of trees is almost pure white birch, and can be seen from the highway or experienced up close on foot. Wandering through an area with white-barked trees as far as the eye can see is an experience unmatched in Pennsylvania.

A STARGAZER'S DRIVE
SNOW SHOE RUN

THE ROUTE

Beginning in Snow Shoe, follow Pennsylvania Highway 144 north and east to Renovo.

In the lingo of astronomers, State Camp—the only town between Snow Shoe and Renovo, and really nothing more than a few camps—has some very "black skies." Translation: There's very little manmade light anywhere near here to interfere with stargazing.

Cherry Springs State Park, thirty miles north of State Camp, has captured the spotlight for viewing stars in Pennsylvania, with its annual Black Forest Star Party each September. But State Camp is also one of the top three sites in the state for studying the cosmos. (The third is the old Potato City Airport, near Coudersport.)

Ambient light from human sources is the bane of amateur astronomers, so the fact that State Camp is a top pick for the stargazers tells you a great deal about this route along Pennsylvania Highway 144. It is the most remote spot in all of Pennsylvania. After leaving the village of Snow Shoe at the southwestern terminus of our tour, there are only very scattered homes and camps until we pull into Renovo at the northeastern end of the trip.

Any time day or night, the drive is packed with wild places and wildlife, but on a clear, black night with the heavens beaming down brighter than most of us have ever seen them, the sheer magnitude of this spot's seclusion is driven right to the core of one's existence. Making the experience even more intense, particularly in the area of the State Camp Overlook, is the open, wind-swept quality of the ridges, given a rooftop-of-the-world feel by the lack of mature trees in the aftermath of a 1985 tornado and 1990 forest fire.

Because of this area's remoteness, the Pennsylvania Game Commission chose it for the 1994 reintroduction of fishers—cat-sized predators that require large expanses of unbroken forest—and the 1998 trap-and-transfer of elk from Elk County to expand that species' range in the state.

All along our Highway 144 route, gravel state forest roads offer side-trips to new sights and adventures. Sproul State Forest, through which this trip runs, has more than three hundred miles of such roads. Vehicle-based wildlife watching, both from Highway 144 and on the gravel roadways, is among the very best that the Keystone State has to offer, particularly for big-woods species like bear, porcupine, and even elk and fisher. The wildflower patches that flourish along the roadsides, in forest clearings, and in the tornado/fire area also make this prime butterfly-watching country from June through August.

Although the two ends of our route are, for our purposes, primarily just starting and finishing lines, Snow Shoe and Renovo are worthy of some scrutiny.

Snow Shoe is one of the region's primary truck stops along Interstate 80 and thus rich in truck-stop culture of diners and quick shops. According to tradition, the village received its name in the eighteenth century when a group of hunters were overtaken by a winter storm and saved themselves with snowshoes they made here from birch saplings. Modern lore holds that the name refers to the locale's reputation as one of the snowiest spots in Pennsylvania.

Renovo is a former railroad town whose glory has passed with that era, marked with a period in 1980, when the Renovo train yards were permanently closed. Even the name of the borough, derived from Latin for "I renew," refers to the complex of massive now-idle railroad repair shops on the east side of town.

Although the first settler, William Baird, came to the site of modern-day Renovo in 1824, the village really started to boom in 1862 when the first Philadelphia and Erie Railroad construction train arrived with workmen and crews, and P&E decided to erect the repair shops here. Land not used by the railroad was laid out as town streets and individual lots for homes.

The casual traveler, moving along the primary routes through town, may jump to the conclusion that there just isn't a business district here. However, just a couple blocks east along Erie Avenue, just before the railroad tracks, stands the remnants of a still-active business district, its off-center location evidence reflecting the strong influence of the town's railroading past.

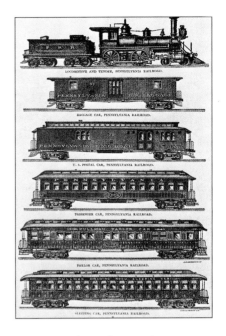

Trains performed many important duties in the Keystone State, whether it be hauling coal, passengers, or the U.S. mail. In the 1880s, the Philadelphia and Erie Railroad used cars similar to the Pennsylvania Railroad equipment pictured here.

LEFT:
A round barn and cornfield stand alongside Pennsylvania Highway 45 in Centre County.

BELOW:
A cardinal flower and daisies grow along Wycoff Run Road in the Quehanna Wilderness Area.

RIGHT:
A restored 1947 8N Ford tractor, pictured on a mountain top in Cameron County, recalls the days of farming past.

FAR RIGHT:
This quaint church can be found in Shintown, just west of Renovo on Highway 120.

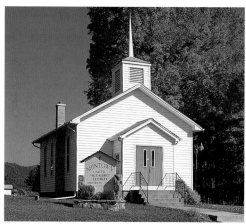

ABOVE:

In Clearfield County, visitors can walk through the peaceful Walker Gardens at Bigler.

LEFT:

An old cemetery with tombstones that date back to the 1800s lies on Airport Road, off Highway 144 in Centre Hall.

Start out at the McElhattan-Rosecrans Reservoir north of Rosecrans and move northwest along Nittany Ridge Road to East End Mountain Road. Travel west on East End Mountain Road, East End Road, and Main Street through Salona to Cedar Springs. From there, drive southwest on Pennsylvania Highway 64 to the intersection with Pennsylvania Highway 26. Follow Highway 26 north to Park View Heights then Pennsylvania Highway 550 west into Bellefonte. Take Pennsylvania Highway 144 south to Highway 26 at Pleasant Gap and follow that west into State College.

Harkening back to their carefree college days, Penn State University alum call this area "Happy Valley." From the perspective of many Penn State graduates, that special zone extends only a mile or two in any direction from the campus, located in State College. Travelers without the benefit of the Penn State experience who rely on a map of the region will instead see it labeled as the Nittany Valley. They'll also notice that it actually extends for many miles to the northeast of Penn State, all the way into Clinton County.

Almost everything in this valley pays tribute to Penn State and its football team, colors of blue and white, mascot the Nittany Lion, or head coach Joe Paterno. The traveler on this tour will see the use of those icons and images grow steadily heavier in business and product names as he or she moves westward from our starting point near the peak of Bald Eagle Mountain to State College.

The broad valley between Bald Eagle Mountain to the north and Nittany Mountain to the south is home to more than Penn State, however, even if much of it has passed its glory days. There's the eerie ghost town of a facility that was the Lamar National Fish Hatchery in the town of Lamar. There's the village of Hecla Park, which in the late 1800s and early 1900s was home to a major amusement park and summer residence that attracted visitors and vacationers from across the state.

Bellefonte, largely overlooked by the mood of modernization in the mid 1900s that destroyed so many historic structures throughout Pennsylvania and elsewhere, is home to one of the largest collections of antebellum and Victorian architecture in the country. Talleyrand Park serves as the gazeboed, arched, and walled center of the historic district. The community also claims the title of home to seven U.S. governors, taking note of direct connections to William Bigler, governor of Pennsylvania, 1852–55; John Bigler, governor of California, 1852–56; Robert J. Walker, governor of the Territory of Kansas, 1857–61; William F. Packer, governor of Pennsylvania, 1858–61; Andrew Gregg Curtin, governor of Pennsylvania, 1861–67; James Addams Beaver, governor of Pennsylvania 1887–91; and Daniel Hastings, governor of Pennsylvania, 1895–99.

There are also diversions to pause a traveler in State College and the adjoining University Park, which is the actual home of Penn State. Fueled by the economy of the university, block after block of State College's downtown is home to specialty shops and eateries catering to every interest and quirk.

University Park, remarkable for the sheer amount of real estate that a major university can consume, is the venue for many major regional exhibitions and performances by top-name entertainers. It's also home to collections housed in facilities ranging from the Palmer Museum of Art to the Frost Entomological (Bug) Museum.

THE NITTANY LION

Symbol of the mighty Penn State sports program, the Nittany Lion is a mountain lion enshrined by the revered statue on the University Park campus and portrayed by a costumed student at sporting events. It was selected as the mascot by the student body in 1906.

The model for the statue, which was dedicated in 1942, was a typical mountain lion. There are some people who believe that the Nittany Lion was modeled after the now-extinct eastern cougar subspecies, once native to Penns Woods, but, there is no evidence to support that claim.

Penn State's lion was dubbed the Nittany Lion because the university is located at the foot of Mount Nittany. That landmass was named for Nita-Nee, an Indian princess in whose honor the Great Spirit formed the mountain.

The Nittany Lion has been Penn State University's mascot for nearly one hundred years.

The Penn State Creamery, part of an ice cream education program at the university that has produced some of today's top ice cream makers, is also worth a stop whenever a traveler hits campus. Flavors unheard of elsewhere wait to be sampled.

AN ECLECTIC TOUR
PENNS AND BUFFALO VALLEYS

Pennsylvania Highway 45 from Lewisburg in Union County to Boalsburg in Centre County takes us through the center of two wide valleys of heavy agriculture bounded both north and south by wooded mountains. The tour can be many things to many travelers, as historic sites, classic architecture, natural wonders, and other tourist opportunities all flourish along this route.

Our trip is first and foremost a recreational shopper's dream. Each little town along the way has its own gathering of specialty shops containing wares that range from quilts and ceramic tiles to Native American crafts and books. Each town has unique restaurants as well, such as Elizabeth's, an upscale bistro in Lewisburg, and the Boalsburg Tavern, with an intimate setting reminiscent of colonial times. Every town also offers at least one antique shop that holds a localized array of Americana. It's the ambience of the communities themselves that really sets the mood for the shopping experience. These are business districts—whether large or small—with tree-lined streets and sidewalks, period lampposts, and

THE ROUTE

From Lewisburg, take Pennsylvania Highway 45 west to Penns Cave Road. Follow that northwest to Penn's Cave, then drive southwest on Pennsylvania Highway 192 to Centre Hall, southeast on Pennsylvania Highway 144 to Old Fort, and southwest on Highway 45 to Boalsburg.

The Lewisburg Hotel is one of the many charming buildings clustered in Lewisburg, a town that offers numerous dining and shopping opportunities.

The Boalsburg Tavern and Restaurant is located at Boalsburg's main intersection.

A road sign in the center of Boalsburg directs travelers to neighboring towns.

ABOVE:

The Reynolds Mansion, a luxurious bed and breakfast, can be found in the heart of Bellefonte's National Register Historic District.

LEFT, TOP:

Woodward Cave offers an hour-long tour along an easy-to-traverse gravel path.

LEFT, BOTTOM:

Tour boats await passengers at the entrance to Penn's Cave.

Colonial brick and Victorian-style buildings with beautifully maintained storefronts, which invite leisurely browsing on foot.

Many places of historical interest lie along this route. Packwood House Museum, built in Lewisburg in the closing years of the eighteenth century, is one of the oldest surviving log structures in the state. Its twenty-seven rooms house a collection of central Pennsylvania Americana from the eighteenth through early twentieth centuries and is right at home in a borough that stages a Victorian Holiday Parade each year in December.

The Mifflinburg Buggy Museum carries the visitor back into the second half of the eighteenth century, when the little community was known as "Buggy Town" for its dominance of the horse-drawn carriage industry. Between 1890 and 1920, Mifflinburg was home to fifty carriage works. The museum is housed in the former home and works of William A. Heiss, and it is one of only seven industrial museums in the country with an original collection on its original site.

Mifflinburg is near the center of the wide Buffalo Valley, where countless roads, streams, mountains, communities, and businesses carry the word "buffalo" in their names. They were christened for the now-gone buffaloes that roamed this region in considerable numbers as late as the second half of the eighteenth century. Just west of Hartleton, Highway 45 leaves the Buffalo Valley to cross Thick Mountain into Penns Valley at Woodward. Like so many other places, Penns Valley traces its name back to Pennsylvania's founder, William Penn.

Boalsburg, where Memorial Day was born in 1864, maintains a monument to the women who created the event by laying flowers on the graves of soldiers who had died in the Civil War. Memorial Day has since grown into an annual, national celebration of community and history. The town is also home to Columbus Chapel, a small stone building that houses the actual chapel of the Christopher Columbus family of Spain; the Boal Mansion; and the Pennsylvania Military Museum, which traces the history of the state and its inhabitants in war. Visitors to the museum are led through a recreated, life-size World War I battlefield, complete with sound effects.

There are also many opportunities for nature lovers along this route. Wildlife watching is bountiful, as all the creatures of the Pennsylvania forest are found in healthy numbers in the section of the Bald Eagle State Forest through which we pass. A prime stop is the state picnic area at Hickernell Springs, in the big woods area a few miles west of Hartleton.

For the slightly more adventurous, tours of Pennsylvania's public caves are available. Two include Woodward Cave, just south of the village of the same name, and the boat-tour of Penns Cave, off Pennsylvania Highway 192 near Centre Hall.

In addition to all the above special features, regulars along this stretch of Highway 45 know it as a prime route for sampling frozen custard. Individual businesses come and go, but for decades, roadside drive-ins at Lewisburg, Mifflinburg, Hartleton, and Millheim have offered constantly changing soft ice cream flavors-of-the-week. The richness of their product makes for a refreshing pause on a hot summer's afternoon.

CAVES OF PENNSYLVANIA

Pennsylvania is home to nine show caves, meaning caves that are open for guided, public tours. Nearly all of them feature underground rooms of varying sizes and formations of stalactites (which drip down from the ceiling) and stalagmites (which grow up from the cave floor and might someday reach the ceiling), but each of the caves also has its own special features.

• Coral Caverns, at Mann's Choice, includes a towering fossil wall, containing the fossil remains of coral and other sea creatures buried more than 400 million years ago when Pennsylvania was under the Great Inland Sea.

• Crystal Cave, near Kutztown, features several large rooms of cave formations.

• Indian Caverns, at Spruce Creek, has produced more than four hundred artifacts from Native Americans who once used portions of the cave.

• The tour of Indian Echo Caverns, west of Hershey near Hummelstown, tells of William Wilson, the hermit who lived inside the caverns for nineteen years after the tragic hanging of his only sister in 1785, and of a "Mystery Box" of strange coins and gems found inside the cave.

• Laurel Caverns, near Uniontown, doesn't have any of the normal cave formations, but it is Pennsylvania's largest public cave.

• Lincoln Caverns, near Huntingdon, offers the most strenuous of the cave tours, with plenty of steep stairs and some very tight-fitting passageways.

• Lost River Caverns, at Hellertown, includes five cavern chambers with an abundance of formations, fluorescent minerals, and an underground stream.

• Penn's Cave, near Centre Hall, is the only cave that is toured by boat. Penns Creek flows through the length of the cave.

• Woodward Cave, near the village of Woodward, is the largest "live" cavern in the state, which means it is still developing. The cave boasts many rare formations, such as helictites, which are stalactites that can grow in any direction and appear to defy gravity.

PART III

POCONOS AND
ENDLESS MOUNTAINS:
THE NORTHEAST

A scenic shoreline flanks the Delaware River at Dingmans Ferry in Pike County.

Ivy covers an old farm building near Tunkhannock.

Northeast Pennsylvania is an incredibly diverse expanse. In different areas of the region the traveler will experience the prosperity of the fastest growing area of the state and the poverty of near-Appalachian conditions, zones of heavy industry and vast regions of rich farmland, rising communities and towns on the backside of their glory days.

Traditions run deep in the northeast. Many fairs, parades, and festivals have been in existence for generations. Landmarks are held in reverence. Historical roots are a blend of different cultures—notably German, English, French, and Welsh—that mingled here during the early European settlement of Pennsylvania.

Although the chain stores and restaurants that are impacting the entire nation are making strong inroads in the northeast, many of them have arrived here later than elsewhere in the state. Here, local concerns remain viable, adding a distinctive feel to travel throughout the region.

SETTLED ADVENTURES
THE UPPER SUSQUEHANNA RIVER

THE ROUTE

At Bloomsburg, drive east on Main Street, then northeast as it becomes Old Berwick Road, northeast on U.S. Highway 11 to West Pittston, and Pennsylvania Highway 92 north and west to Tunkhannock. From there take Pennsylvania Highway 29 south and west to State Route 3003, Route 3003 north to North Mehoopany, State Route 4002 north to Township Road 443, and 443 northwest to State Route 3001, which runs northwest to Laceyville.

The following route is probably the least "back" of the backroads presented in this book. The traveler is on major highways or in towns for nearly the entire trip, witnessing how Pennsylvania communities have related to the state's greatest river, the mighty Susquehanna. For this route, look beyond Pennsylvania's wildlife and beautiful scenes of natural wonders. Instead, see how the communities have arranged themselves in relation to the Susquehanna: older streets and parks along the riverbanks, with plenty of access to the water, and newer streets and business districts farther removed from the river. At the edges of the business districts stand the larger, often now-vacant, industrial buildings. Newer neighborhoods of single-family homes form the next outer layer, often followed by commercial strips of shopping centers, chain restaurants, motels, and convenience stores. The history of development in these communities is clearly told by this layout.

Bloomsburg, the only community in Pennsylvania officially incorporated as a town, has a vibrant and flourishing downtown made up of more than 650 buildings designated on the National Register of Historic Places. The downtown is aided economically by the local college, Bloomsburg University, which was founded in 1839 as the Bloomsburg Literary Institute and today enrolls more than seventy-five hundred students. That influx of college students has a big impact on a town with a population of twelve thousand and naturally leads to an eclectic mix of more than eighty businesses, shops, and restaurants.

However, one gets the distinct impression that downtown Bloomsburg, unlike some college towns, would be doing just fine even if the university were located elsewhere. It's the kind of place that hosts major arts and crafts shows in the spring and summer, and TreeFest, a festival of more

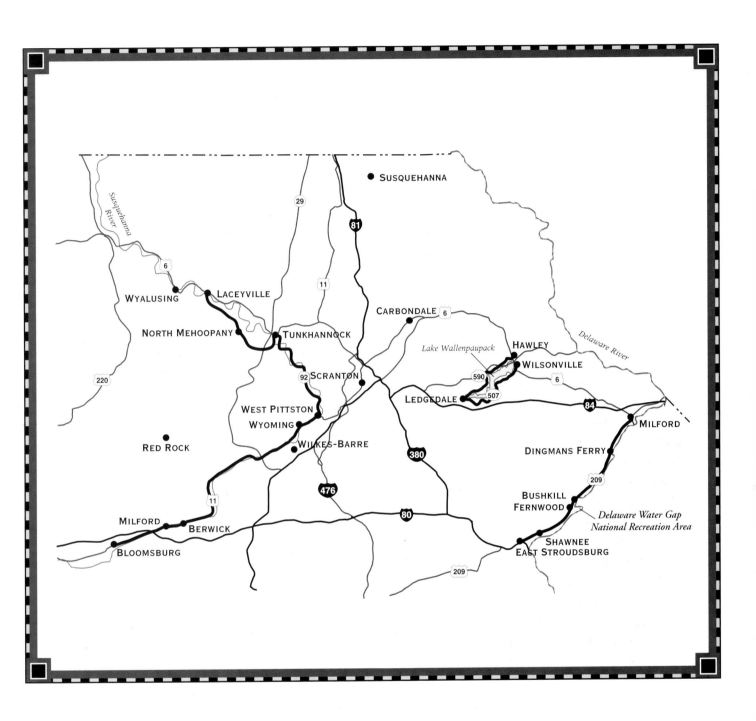

LEFT:

Northeastern Pennsylvania shows its colors in this breathtaking autumn view north of Red Rock in Sullivan County.

ABOVE:

A saw-whet owl perches in a thicket. Not much bigger than a common robin, the saw-whet owl is Pennsylvania's smallest owl species.

than one hundred beautifully decorated Christmas trees in late November and early December. The town is home to a twenty-five-year-old resident theater company, the Bloomsburg Theatre Ensemble, considered a leader among professional theaters in the state. And, it's home to the largest fair in Pennsylvania. The Bloomsburg Fair, hitting its 150th year in 2004, draws big-name entertainment and about a half-million visitors to the 234-acre, twenty-building fairgrounds just outside of town the third week of each September.

Berwick, northeast of Bloomsburg on our route, is a half-dozen miles from the gigantic twin cooling towers of the Pennsylvania Power & Light Company's nuclear power plant. The 540-foot-tall columns of concrete and the clouds of steam they press heavenward are the dominant feature on the town's landscape when seen from a distance. Up close there are other features to draw the traveler's attention. On Market Street, Jackson Park surrounds City Hall in the former Jackson Mansion, a century-old Victorian designed by Colonel Clarence G. Jackson while held in a Confederate prison during the Civil War. Completed in 1878, the building is made of Vermont stone and features hand-carved woodwork, tiled fireplaces, and massive entrances. There's also Berwick Industries, the world's largest manufacturer of decorative ribbons and bows since 1945, which stands on Bomboy Lane.

The Susquehanna Riverlands at Berwick is a twelve-thousand-acre nature preserve and outdoor education center along both the west and east shores of the Susquehanna River. It has been designated one of Pennsylvania's seventy-one Important Bird Areas by the National Audubon Society. Although this route is generally urban, the Riverlands offer a welcome touch of nature. The last quarter of our tour will return to nature as well, as the Susquehanna uncharacteristically meanders for several miles through northern Wyoming County. There, the passing landscape alternates between tall mountains and large flat river bottoms with names like The Neck, Jayne Bend, and Quicks Bend.

Another highlight of this route can be found in Wyoming, near Wilkes-Barre. Swetland Homestead, built circa 1803, is a cabin that over the years was enlarged into a stately Victorian home by the prospering Swetland family. Today it's a museum featuring period rooms that span seventy years and illustrating the changes in living spaces and furnishings of a growing America.

At the end of our route, in Laceyville, the most notable piece of history is a three-story building on Main Street known as the Oldest House. Built in 1781 as a stop for canal boats on the Susquehanna River, it is said to be the most ancient frame house in the Endless Mountains, the region of the state north and east of this point.

AROUND THE LAKE
LAKE WALLENPAUPACK

Lake Wallenpaupack, the third-largest manmade lake in Pennsylvania, is a lake with two faces. Most travelers, and locals for that matter, know the very public eastern face on the Pike County side of the lake. Much less traveled and usually overlooked is the wilder western face on the Wayne County shore. This tour explores both sides of the Poconos attraction.

Pennsylvania Power & Light Company built the lake in 1926 as a hydroelectric power source. The lake, 13.5 miles long with 5,700 acres of water surface and 52 miles of shoreline, was created by damming Wallenpaupack Creek. The Leni Lenape Indians gave the stream its name, which means "the stream of swift and slow water."

PP&L has developed six recreation areas, three natural areas, and several observation areas, featuring hundreds of acres of forest lands, wildlife, walking trails, campsites, and boat slips around Lake Wallenpaupack. We'll pass by all of the developments on our route.

Tafton Dike Observation Area is a good place to get acquainted with the area. Built on an earth-and-stone dike near the intersection of U.S. Highway 6 and Pennsylvania Highway 507, it offers a view of the lake that stretches to the horizon, as well as a map of the lake and the surrounding region.

The Lake Wallenpaupack Overlook is a scenic point along Pennsylvania Highway 590 next to the Wallenpaupack Dam. It offers another great view of the bulk of the lake, a permanent map of the region, and active osprey nest platforms.

The three-hundred-acre Shuman Point Natural Area, near Hawley, is one of the last undeveloped areas in this land of resorts and multi-million-dollar summer homes. A trail leads through part of the area, much of it along the shoreline. Adjacent to Shuman Point is the sixty-acre Beech House Creek Wildlife Refuge, a wetland area of beaver activity and waterfowl nesting. Nearby Caffrey Camping Area offers both tent and trailer camping sites.

The Lacawac Sanctuary Foundation, a private, nonprofit nature preserve, is located on the southwestern shore of Lake Wallenpaupack. The foundation's primary purposes are to protect Lake Lacawac, a fifty-three-acre glacial lake and bog system, and its watershed area about a mile from Lake Wallenpaupack, and to provide an area for scientific research and community education.

Camping sites and picnic areas thrive around Lake Wallenpaupack. Five Mile Point is a youth-group-only camping site, with boat-in and walk-in lakefront sites. Ledgedale Camping Area offers more tent and trailer sites, and the adjacent eighty-acre woodland of the Ledgedale Natural

THE ROUTE

From Hawley, follow Pennsylvania Highway 590 southwest to State Route 2002. Drive southwest on 2002, south on State Route 3015, west on State Route 3008, and southwest on State Route 3013 to Ledgedale. Follow Ledgedale Road south to Pennsylvania Highway 507, and take it northeast around the lake to Wilsonville.

*The sky and water are both a brilliant blue in this view
of Decker Pond, near Wilsonville in Pike County.*

RIGHT:
An airboat rests at the edge of the Susquehanna River.

The Tunkhannock Viaduct, near Nicholson, is 2,375 feet long and rises 240 feet above Tunkhannock Creek. The reinforced concrete structure, designed for the Delaware Lackawanna & Western Railroad, was the largest of its kind when it went into service in 1915. Novelist Theodore Dreiser called it "one of the true wonders of the world."

FAR LEFT:
A bear crossing sign cautions travelers to be alert.

LEFT:
Black bears are on the increase in Pennsylvania, and the swamps of Pike County are prime habitat. Here, three bear cubs nuzzle their mother.

The Lackawanna Railroad touts the Pocono Mountains as "one of the most alluring resorts for health and pleasure to be found in the east" in this 1902 magazine ad.

Area provides hiking and nature-watching opportunities. On the southern shore, near Burns and Kipp Islands, is the Ironwood Point Camping Area, another tent and trailer facility, which includes twelve lakefront sites for walk-in camping. Four islands in the lake—Epply, Kipp, Burns, and Cairns—offer grills and tables for boat-in picnicking. All but Burns have summer-use restroom facilities. Near the end of our tour sits the Wilsonville Camping Area, PP&L's largest lakeside campground with 160 sites.

Although most of our route lies among a wide range of private vacation homes and cabins, PP&L owns most of the shoreline and the lake itself. With the utility's ring of recreational facilities, marinas, and available boat rentals there is plenty of public access.

Lake Wallenpaupack is largely a boating culture. You can view the lake and its attractions from the roadside, but if you bring or rent a boat you'll get an entirely different perspective. There are also a few companies that take boat tours out several times a day during the tourist season. One of these takes place on the forty-eight-foot, wooden *Spirit of Paupack,* which began life as a whale-watching boat along the coast of Maine in 1960 and has sunk twice in Wallenpaupack. It's been restored and is entirely lake-worthy now.

When driving the route around Lake Wallenpaupack, pay attention to the charming towns that surround it. Hawley, which is actually a mile north of the lake, is too good to miss when visiting this region. Much of the Victorian town's period architecture now houses a diverse array of antique shops, artists' galleries, specialty stores, and restaurants. The period is further celebrated each December in the community's Winterfest, which features a nonmotorized Victorian parade, Victorian costume gala, and Victorian tea, along with events like ice carvings and holiday readings.

Highway 507, which leads into Wilsonville and then back to Hawley, at the end of our route, is home to several large resorts, hotels, and motels, but many period inns and bed and breakfasts are also available in Hawley. The star of these is the Settler's Inn at Bingham Park, a refurbished hotel built in the grand style of 1927. The restaurant at the inn is known for its regional cuisine, featuring locally grown and produced ingredients.

There are two prime times of day for making the drive around Lake Wallenpaupack, so choose wisely before you go. Early morning presents views of the lake with the least amount of heat-induced haze. Early evening is the wildife watcher's favorite time to make the trip. The huge amounts of land around the lake closed to the public—and hunters—have led to enormous deer and bear populations that typically begin their nightly travels in the evening.

ABOVE:

Steer skulls decorate the side of the Phoenix Antique Shop on Highway 209 in Pike County.

FACING PAGE:

Kitchen Creek rushes through northeastern Pennsylvania's Luzerne County on a foggy spring morning.

THROUGH THE APPALACHIAN MOUNTAINS
THE DELAWARE WATER GAP

THE ROUTE

Drive northeast on U.S. Highway 209 from East Stroudsburg to Shawnee, northeast on State Routes 2032 and 2028 (River Road) to Fernwood, and north on U.S. 209 to Milford.

Nowhere else in Pennsylvania comes as close to mimicking the rough-hewn scenery of the wild American West as the Delaware Water Gap. Here, the broad and, in places, rambunctious Delaware River slices through the Appalachian Mountains. Sheer cliff walls press up against the river. Trees cling to the sharply rising sides of the mountains. And, although U.S. Highway 209—the primary route through the region—does clog with traffic at times, particularly weekends and holidays, spots devoid of civilization can still be found.

The National Park Service has designated the forty miles of river corridor from the town of Delaware Water Gap north to Milford as the Delaware Water Gap National Recreation Area and the corresponding section of the Delaware River as a national scenic river. In addition to the forty miles of the middle Delaware River, which is the only remaining undammed river in the eastern United States, the park preserves almost seventy thousand acres of ridges, forests, lakes, and streams along the Delaware's New Jersey and Pennsylvania shores.

Throughout the national recreation area, historic farmhouses and agricultural fields make the landscape appear much as it did in the 1800s. However, the Gap area along the river has proven to be an archeological treasure of period after period, offering an unbroken chain of finds dating all the way back to 8500 B.C.

This is also the easternmost extent of the Pocono Mountains, the fabled region of massive resorts, tourist attractions, and amusement parks. Locally, the Kittatinny was the first of the resort hotels at Delaware Water Gap. Named for the Kittatinny Ridge, it opened in 1832 to a capacity of 25 guests and grew to accommodate more than 250 vacationers at a time by the end of the Civil War. In the early 1900s, changing vacation styles—brought on largely by the automobile—directed tourists away from the traditional fresh air and scenery of the Gap, and the area's fifteen operating resort hotels were soon destined to close their doors.

While East Stroudsburg is technically not part of the Delaware Water Gap or the national recreation area, it does offer a nice beginning for our tour, with its college-town business district and streets flanked with trees. From its beginning in East Stroudsburg, this entire tour is a mix of towns and villages lined with unique stores, antique shops, and tourist attractions, interspersed with wide expanses of natural wonders.

Scenic waterfalls are regular sights along this route that cuts across many streams on their descent to the Delaware River, but the village of Bushkill is the region's epicenter for water cascading through steep and rocky drops. Just outside town lies Bushkill Falls, an area that features trails leading to various views of eight impressive waterfalls, the largest being the 100-foot-tall Main Falls. Other top-rated waterfalls along our route are 75-foot Dingmans Falls and 70-foot Silver Thread Falls, both near the village of Dingmans Ferry, and the 105-foot-tall, three-section Raymondskill Falls, a couple miles south of Milford.

One of the few bridges across the Delaware in this region is found at Dingmans Ferry, which from 1735 to the present has been home to either a ferry or a bridge. Andrew Dingman established the first ferry here in 1735, along with a settlement that he named Dingmans Choice. The U.S. Postal Service changed the name to Dingmans Ferry when it opened a local office in 1868. The current bridge is the fourth to stand here. It was built around 1900 and remains one of a very few privately owned toll bridges in the country.

Mining was a way of life in northeastern Pennsylvania. These images were taken at the mines near Wilkes-Barre.

Milford, the northern terminus of our drive, may have been named for the many mills working there (nine at one point in the early 1800s), but today it's a center of history and retail. Grey Towers National Historic Landmark—former home to Gifford Pinchot, twice governor of Pennsylvania and father of American conservation—features gardens that have been restored to reflect Pinchot's gardens in the 1930s and 1940s. Pike County Historical Society's Columns Museum in Milford houses the Mayflower Candlestick, an original that was brought to America on the Mayflower in 1620, and the blood-stained Lincoln Flag—the very one that cradled President Lincoln's head minutes after his assassination in 1865. Between those two sites lies historic downtown Milford, an area of tree-lined streets, buildings constructed in the early 1800s with locally mined bluestone, and many shops and galleries to peruse.

PART IV

DEEP HISTORY AND DIVERSE CULTURES: THE SOUTHEAST

FACING PAGE:

Nodding daffodils and a stone farmhouse stand beside a meandering stream in Lancaster County.

ABOVE:

An Amish family travels the backroads of Pennsylvania by horse and buggy.

The southeast corner of Pennsylvania holds the greatest concentration of humanity in the state. Tall cities, like Philadelphia, Allentown, and Reading, rise from the countryside, and suburban sprawl spreads farther into the former agricultural areas with each passing year. Nevertheless, pockets of wonderful rural life and even outright wildness have managed to survive. The southeast corner also maintains a scattering of small towns, most with strong connections to long history.

The region is a melting pot of different cultures, some of long standing, others of more recent vintage. English, German, Scotch-Irish, Swiss, and Welsh all settled southeastern Pennsylvania in large numbers. Although all heritages are still represented here, it's the Amish, Mennonites, and other Pennsylvania Dutch descendents that have captured the most attention of the modern visitor.

It's a geographically diverse region as well, from the beginning of a coastal plain in Philadelphia and Delaware Counties, through the fox-chase hillsides of Bucks County, across the rich farmlands of Berks, Lancaster, and Lebanon Counties, to the southernmost edge of the Appalachian Mountain range in Lehigh and Schuylkill Counties. The routes in this section will lead the traveler through some of the very best areas southeastern Pennsylvania has to offer.

PENNSYLVANIA FARMLAND
HEGINS VALLEY

THE ROUTE

Beginning in Taylorville, follow State Route 4020 (Deep Creek Road) southwest, then Pennsylvania Highway 125 south to Hegins. From there, take Pennsylvania Highway 25 west to Berrysburg.

While regions in Pennsylvania a bit farther south have a stronger reputation for agricultural production, few of them match the Hegins Valley of Schuylkill and Dauphin Counties for pure farmland as far as the eye can see. Nearly every agricultural commodity produced in Pennsylvania is grown somewhere in the broad valley that lies between Mahantango and Broad Mountains in the east and Berry Mountain in the west.

Everything from potatoes to grapes to hogs are grown or raised by the farm families that have occupied these lands for generations. That diversity of products is reflected in the many roadside produce stands that line this route, which sell their wares both fresh and processed into a wondrous array of treats, like pies or a dried apple ring known as "schnitz."

Although the communities of the Hegins Valley were consolidated into two area school districts many years ago, the one-room schoolhouses that formerly served their educational needs are a regular sight along this route. They've been converted into everything from residences to day-care facilities to a garden center.

The valley, and more precisely the mountains that border it, also lies very firmly in the hard coal region of Pennsylvania. Mining has been a major industry here through nearly as many generations as has farming. Taylorville, the beginning of our trip at the intersection of Pennsylvania Highway 901 and Deep Creek Road, was the site of a colliery that operated off and on from 1855 to 1933. The village's proximity to travel routes

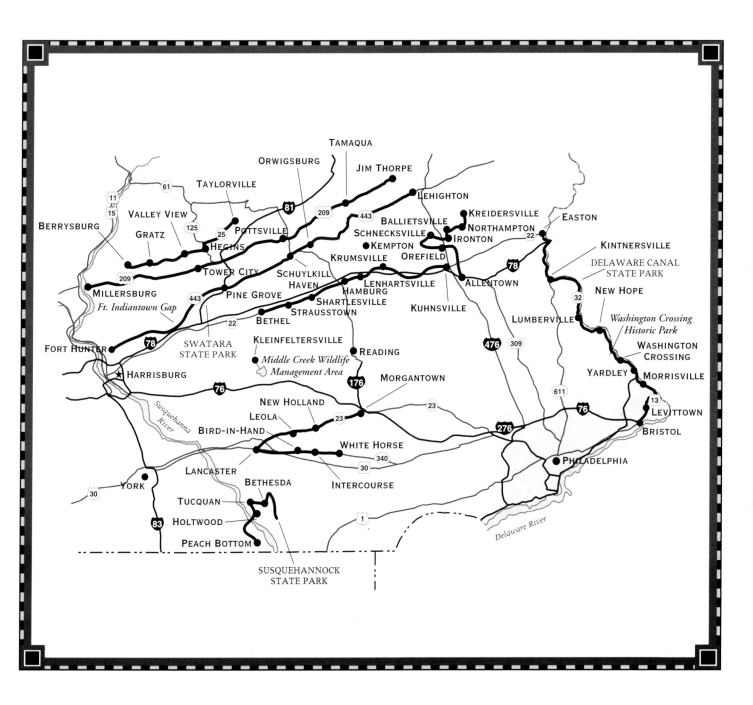

TAMAQUA
ORWIGSBURG
JIM THORPE
TAYLORVILLE
61
LEHIGHTON
11
15
KREIDERSVILLE
EASTON
VALLEY VIEW
BALLIETSVILLE
NORTHAMPTON
BERRYSBURG
209
SCHNECKSVILLE
IRONTON
22
KINTNERSVILLE
GRATZ
125
25
POTTSVILLE
KEMPTON
OREFIELD
DELAWARE CANAL
HEGINS
KRUMSVILLE
STATE PARK
209
NEW HOPE
TOWER CITY
32
443
SCHUYLKILL
LENHARTSVILLE
ALLENTOWN
Washington Crossing
MILLERSBURG
HAVEN
HAMBURG
78
Historic Park
Ft. Indiantown Gap
PINE GROVE
SHARTLESVILLE
KUHNSVILLE
LUMBERVILLE
WASHINGTON
22
STRAUSSTOWN
CROSSING
BETHEL
YARDLEY
MORRISVILLE
78
KLEINFELTERSVILLE
SWATARA
476
309
STATE PARK
Middle Creek Wildlife
READING
13
FORT HUNTER
Management Area
611
LEVITTOWN
176
MORGANTOWN
76
HARRISBURG
BRISTOL
76
NEW HOLLAND
23
276
Susquehanna
LEOLA
23
River
BIRD-IN-HAND
PHILADELPHIA
WHITE HORSE
LANCASTER
340
30
YORK
BETHESDA
INTERCOURSE
30
TUCQUAN
HOLTWOOD
1
83
Delaware River
PEACH BOTTOM

SUSQUEHANNOCK
STATE PARK

OVERLEAF:
Rolling farmland sweeps across southeastern Pennsylvania.

between some of the first major communities to develop in the region made it a starting point for many of the settlers that flowed into the Hegins Valley.

With some exceptions, Valley View—which can seem to be part of Hegins, as the two towns have merged in the Tri-Valley Area High School neighborhood—has been the eastern Hegins Valley commercial district for the past few decades. Most of the restaurants, stores, and offices that remain in the area today are found here, with the ever-present farmlands just out their backdoors. History is important here, as can be witnessed in the homemade memorial to miners that fills the front yard of one residence along Pennsylvania Highway 25.

The coal region of southeastern Pennsylvania provided jobs for many local residents. In this image from 1912, a coal miner and rail car exit Short Mountain Slope.

Gratz is home to the two landmarks most widely known outside the valley: the Gratz Fair and the Crossroads Sale and Market. Launched in 1873, the Gratz Fair is one of the region's longest-running country fairs. With strong and long-standing ties to its agricultural beginnings, it has an air of permanence that many more-modern events and celebrations seem to lack. New generations of fair-goers are introduced annually to the wonders of hand-preserved jams and jellies, locally grown giants of the pumpkin and squash world, and carefully crafted quilts and furniture. In 1905, however, when it seemed that organizers could no longer raise enough money through the event to pay the bills, it looked like the fair would cease. A local business stepped forward, took over the fair on a two-year trial basis, and added new amusements to bring renewed interest to the fair. Those efforts led to the fair's success, now operational for over one hundred years and running.

The Crossroads Sale and Market, just west of the borough of Gratz, is a weekly farmers' market with few rivals for sheer magnitude in Pennsylvania. Since its beginning in 1931, each Friday the market's twenty-one thousand square feet of sale space is occupied by about seventy vendors of local produce and manufacture. Some families have had regular booths here since the Crossroads' inception. Other families have been shoppers for nearly as long. On particularly busy Fridays, the parking lots have been known to hold as many as two thousand vehicles.

Berrysburg, the western terminus of this tour, is one of the smallest boroughs in Pennsylvania, with about 350 residents. Its wide, tree-lined streets and broad-windowed storefronts, which have now been converted to residential use, speak to another era that beckons many of us.

THE HARD COAL REGION
FROM MINING TOWNS TO THE MILLERSBURG FERRY

A drive through Pennsylvania's hard coal region on U.S. Highway 209 is a tour of glory days long gone. The coal industry, which brought many families to the area, is a shadow of the employer it was in the first half of the twentieth century. Jobs that kept three and four garment factories at peak operation in many of the regional towns have mostly migrated overseas. Downtown five-and-dime and mom-and-pop grocery stores have faded and disappeared with their customer base.

Although the overall trend has been downward for several decades—and it continues in that direction—it isn't an even decline. Here and there, plenty of bright spots spring out as local entrepreneurs find niches to fill with specialty stores, light industry, and the occasional tech operation. The readily available storefronts adapt as easily to their new coats of paint as to their new occupants. It's an ongoing tale of boom and bust, ready to be studied as we drive through these towns. Watch the storefronts—that's where you'll find the story.

It's also a tale told in the scars on the land. Mining leaves a big and heavy footprint, in the form of towering mountains of slag material removed from the mines to get at precious anthracite; streams turned orange from sulfur released by burrowing deep down into the earth; and old railroad beds minus the tracks that once were the coal "pipeline" out of the region. These monuments to coal mining's heyday line most of our route. Many may be hidden by the recovering landscape of new trees, but they're still there. Pause, look a bit deeper, and you will see.

Not all the towns along our route have suffered to the same degree. Jim Thorpe, renamed in 1953 from Mauch Chunk and East Mauch Chunk in honor of the Native American athlete who gained fame in the 1912 Olympics, has maintained a bustling tourist district based on railroading history, river rafting, mountain biking, and

THE ROUTE

From Jim Thorpe, drive west on U.S. Highway 209 to Millersburg.

Jim Thorpe, who excelled as an Olympian, football player, and baseball player, is considered one of the greatest athletes of the twentieth century.

An antique Oldsmobile gas pump near New Mahoning in Carbon County is a reminder of days gone by.

Colorful cabooses rest at the train station in the town of Jim Thorpe.

The Millersburg Ferry is the last ferry to still cross the Susquehanna River today. Swinging open the signal door lets ferry operators know you are waiting for a ride.

Old signs grace the side of a barn in Carbon County.

THE NED SMITH LEGACY

The existing Ned Smith Center for Nature & Art in Millersburg will soon be replaced by a new building just east of town.

"Future home of the Ned Smith Center for Nature & Art" reads the sign on a grassy knoll just east of Millersburg.

For several years, a growing cadre of volunteers from the local community and wildlife art enthusiasts from across Pennsylvania have worked to raise the several million dollars needed to erect a combination art gallery/nature center/education facility in the name of the late Ned Smith. Ground was broken in 2003.

E. Stanley "Ned" Smith, born in Millersburg in 1919, was one of the most widely published wildlife artists at the time of his death in 1985. His paintings and sketchwork are noted for unrivaled accuracy in depicting native Pennsylvania wildlife in its natural setting. He was also a revered, if self-taught, naturalist and writer, whose observations in works such as *Gone for the Day* are considered classics of the genre.

arts festivals. The shops and restaurants of the Victorian-era downtown cluster around the New Jersey Central Railroad Station, which has been restored and converted into an information center. At the eastern edge of town lies the final resting place of the athlete Jim Thorpe, who had never visited the area while alive.

In recent years, Tamaqua and Pottsville have enjoyed a slight resurgence, powered by local commerce. Pottsville, the county seat of Schuylkill County, also has much to offer in the way of historical interest. Founded in 1831, Yuengling Brewery is America's oldest brewery, currently operated by fifth-generation Yuenglings. Several markers around the city catalog points in the life of John O'Hara, a native son who became one of the greatest short story writers of the twentieth century. He regularly wrote about 1920s Pottsville socialites in his "Gibbsville" stories. The Garfield Diner, a 1950s art deco restaurant, was featured as an example of vanishing Americana in a PBS documentary on diners. Murals on and in many of the downtown buildings illustrate street scenes and buildings from another era. The Jewish Museum of Eastern Pennsylvania is home to a collection of artifacts from the local Jewish community.

Millersburg, the end of our tour, has maintained its prosperity to a much greater degree and much more consistently than most towns in Pennsylvania. If there is an ideal of the American small town, it's Millersburg. Wide, tree-canopied sidewalks wind among the stores and shops of an active retail center.

Also at this spot, the Millersburg Ferry, which has functioned in one form or another since at least the 1820s, still shuttles vehicles and people across the mighty Susquehanna River. Operated today by the Millersburg Ferry Boat Association, the ferry runs with two stern-paddle-wheel boats—the *Roaring Bull* and the *Falcon*—each capable of carrying as many as four cars and sixty passengers. A crossing of the river takes twenty to thirty minutes.

SMALL-TOWN PENNSYLVANIA
HIGHWAY 443 THROUGH THE BLUE MOUNTAINS

Although this route has its share of special attractions, it's most notable for the many wonderfully average small towns through which it passes. Most have their historic highlights and shopping districts, but none have developed into tourist towns. The eateries similarly offer good food, sometimes with a local flair, but nothing much out of the mainstream. In short, this is small-town Pennsylvania.

With that caveat behind us, I will immediately contradict it with the first few spots along our tour. Fort Hunter isn't much of a town today, but it is home to Fort Hunter Mansion and Park, the site of one of the small forts erected by the British from Harrisburg to Sunbury just before the French and Indian War. The original structure was a ten-foot-by-fourteen-foot log blockhouse surrounded by a stockade, but in the nineteenth century, the site was developed into a sprawling riverside plantation, complete with the mansion that exists as a museum today.

Between Fort Hunter and Fort Indiantown Gap lies an area of large horse farms that has developed around Penn National Race Course, where thoroughbreds have run year-round since 1972. The main track is a one-mile oval, but in 1978 Penn National debuted the first turf course in Pennsylvania.

For thousands of years, Native Americans—including those against whom structures like Fort Hunter were erected—lived on and farmed the area of the Blue Mountains that today is known as Indiantown Gap. Although raiding parties passed through the gap in the mid 1700s, those Native American warriors could never have imagined the massive military applications this tract of land would have today.

The nineteen-thousand-acre Fort Indiantown Gap is headquarters to the Pennsylvania Department of Military Affairs and the Pennsylvania National Guard. Also located at "The Gap" is the Eastern Army Aviation Training Site, the second-largest helicopter training facility in the United States, and the seven-hundred-acre Indiantown Gap National Cemetery, which lays to rest an average of five former service members or their spouses each day. Although the thirteen hundred buildings of the facility saw much more use during World War II, the Korean War, and the Vietnam

From Fort Hunter, just north of Harrisburg, take Pennsylvania Highway 443 east to Lehighton.

The silhouette of an Amish barn stands against the backdrop of a dramatic sunset.

Conflict, and when some of them were used as a Cuban refugee center in 1980, about 170,000 transient soldiers use the 170 firing ranges and training areas each year. (At one point in this section of our tour, a well-signed tank-training course crosses Pennsylvania Highway 443.) In addition, the sprawling acreage is a major site of outdoor recreation, with much of its land open to public hunting and fishing. Nature conservation is also practiced, as 158 acres have been set aside to protect the only known colony of regal fritillary butterflies east of the Mississippi River.

A couple miles east of Fort Indiantown Gap, Pennsylvania Highway 443 passes between a small church and its cemetery. This is the Moonshine Church and Cemetery, begun as a free burial ground in 1822 by Henry Moonshine. The original church, a log structure erected in the 1830s, was burned to the ground in 1961 and has since been rebuilt. The cemetery, where Joseph Raber (victim of the infamous group of local murderers named the Blue-Eyed Six) was buried 1878, is a favored site of Pennsylvania paranormal investigators.

A few miles farther east lies the largely undeveloped 3,515 acres of the Swatara State Park. The land was acquired between 1971 and 1987 with plans to develop a 752-acre lake complete with nearby campsites and other recreational facilities. Fortunately for the many wetlands and unique ecosystems on the site, the state has never been able to move ahead with the plans.

Among the first communities we encounter as we pass from Lebanon County into Schuylkill County is the borough of Pine Grove, which is officially designated a National Historic District due to the bungalow-craftsman, late-Victorian, and Federal architectural styles featured in the various 233 buildings within its 1,770 acres.

Schuylkill Haven has earned the designation as "The Little Town That Could" for its Borough Day in late September each year. From early morning to the fireworks-lit night, volunteer organizations and professional street performers stage the most event-packed day for any community in the country this size (population, about fifty-five hundred).

Of all the small towns along this route, Orwigsburg has maintained the most active and filled downtown business district, attracting a considerable number of new specialty shops and keeping traditional anchors, such as a true five-and-dime.

Along the last leg of our route, just before Lehighton, stands the JEM Classic Car Museum, showcasing the private collection of more than forty automobiles and motorcycles, from a 1902 Curved Dash Olds to a 1962 Corvette. The eighteen thousand square feet of exhibit space is operated as a public museum today.

BRIDGES AND BACKROADS
THE LEHIGH VALLEY COVERED BRIDGE TOUR

Covered bridge tours are not hard to come by in Pennsylvania, where 250 of the 1,500 remaining covered bridges in the United States are found. Several tourist promotion agencies in various regions of the state have charted routes connecting covered bridges within their areas, and some like the Lehigh Valley Convention and Visitors Bureau have even placed signage along the routes.

The Lehigh Valley tour is unique in that it runs through a major metropolitan area, providing an insightful contrast between the romance of the covered bridges and the frenzy of the modern world. It also offers a few special sights along its route not related to the bridges.

Bogert's Bridge, spanning the Little Lehigh River 1.1 miles from the intersection of Martin Luther King Jr. Drive and Oxford Drive, is the first bridge of the tour. The 145-foot-long single span—one of the oldest in the country—was built in 1841 and saved by local residents from demolition in 1956 after a truck damaged it. Today it is for foot traffic only.

As our route follows Fish Hatchery Road to the next bridge, it first carries the traveler past the Lenni Lenape Museum of Indian Culture. Renovated in 2002, this is the site of several Native American events, like the annual October Festival. We also pass the Lil-Le-Hi Trout Nursery, a facility for raising fish operated by the Queen City Sportsmen. The hatchery warrants a stop by anyone who marvels at large trout and plenty of them. Kids can spend considerable time tossing fish pellets to the eager swarms.

Our route next moves along Cedar Crest Boulevard, passing several varied shopping districts and Dorney Park & Wildwater Kingdom. The park, which today features one hundred rides on two hundred acres, began in 1860 as a fish hatchery along Cedar Creek and evolved into a summer resort area, with games, playground, hotel, and small zoo. A carousel was added in the early years of the twentieth century, followed by a miniature train to take guests on tours of the park in 1935. The real ride-building boom started in the 1970s, and a water park was added in 1985.

Continue on Cedar Crest to the intersection with Iron Bridge Road, a left onto which will take the traveler to the Manasses Guth (Guth's) Bridge, a 120-foot-long single span over Jordan Creek. It was built in 1858. Next up is Wehr's Bridge (also known as Seiger's Bridge), built over Jordan Creek in 1841, the 140-foot-long single span is today part of Whitehall Township's Covered Bridge Park, a nice quiet spot for a picnic. Also spanning the Jordan is Rex's Bridge. At 150 feet long, it is the longest covered bridge in the Lehigh Valley. It was also built in 1858. Geiger's Bridge, the fourth covered bridge stretching over Jordan Creek, is the third structure on our tour built in 1858. It measures 120 feet end to end. Schlicher's Bridge, the shortest covered bridge on the tour at 108 feet in length, is also the newest. The single-span structure was built in 1882.

THE ROUTE

Begin at the intersection of Martin Luther King Jr. Drive and Oxford Drive in Allentown. Turn left on Oxford Drive to Bogert's Bridge, left onto Lehigh Parkway, right onto Fish Hatchery Road, right onto Cedar Crest Boulevard, and left onto Iron Bridge Road across Manasses Guth Bridge. Turn left onto River Road to Wehr's Bridge, left onto Parkland Terrace, and right onto Pennsylvania Highway 309. In Orefield, take a left onto Kernsville Road, right onto Jordan Road, and cross Rex's Bridge. From there, turn right onto Jordan Road to Geiger's Bridge, right on Rhueton Hill Road, cross Schlicher's Bridge, turn right onto Highway 309 to Schnecksville, and left onto Sand Springs Road. Continue to Ironton, then turn left onto Mauch Chunk Road, and follow it to Ballietsville. Finally, turn right onto Pennsylvania Highway 329 to Northampton, then left on Kreidersville Road, which leads to Kreidersville.

ABOVE:

Schlicher's Bridge, built in 1882, is the "newest" of the Lehigh Valley's covered bridges. Why are the bridges covered? According to an old, local quip, "The bridges are covered for the same reason our womenfolk wear long dresses. It protects the structure underneath that is seldom seen but appreciated just the same."

RIGHT:

The structure of truss work inside Schlicher's Covered Bridge shows sturdy construction.

The Dreibelbis Station Bridge in Berks County was built in 1869. It is 172 feet long and 16 feet wide.

FAR LEFT:
The owner of this 1935 Model 2025 Rolls Royce travels in style down a farm lane in southeastern Pennsylvania.

LEFT:
A dilapidated Imperial gas pump on Old Route 22 is a relic of days gone by in Shartlesville.

WILDLANDS CONSERVANCY

A couple miles south of the Lehigh Valley Covered Bridge Tour lies the home of the Wildlands Conservancy, a nonprofit, member-supported organization that has purchased and saved more than thirty-one thousand acres of wild space in Pennsylvania.

On the banks of Little Lehigh Creek, just off Orchid Place on the northern edge of Emmaus, the conservancy headquarters itself at the seventy-two-acre Pool Wildlife Sanctuary. Entrusted to the conservancy in 1975 by the late Leonard Parker Pool, founder of Air Products and Chemicals, the sanctuary features an array of nature trails through various ecosystems, a collection of native Pennsylvania trees, an environmental education center with children's discovery room and lending library, a wildflower meadow, and a year-round schedule of special nature events and festivals.

Near Schlicher's is the entrance to the Trexler-Lehigh County Game Preserve, founded in 1906 by local industrialist General Harry C. Trexler in an effort to conserve the bison and elk of the American West. The twelve-hundred-acre park was at first a drive-through attraction, where the big game animals roamed across large fenced areas. A children's zoo was added in 1974, but it wasn't until 1994 that major expansion and changes began. Today the preserve is home to more than 230 animals of fifty species and includes nature trails, concessions, pony rides, and the popular drive-through areas of bison and elk.

Kreidersville Bridge, the final covered span on our tour, is Northampton County's only remaining covered bridge. Its 116-foot-long span extends over the Hokendauqua Creek. Built in 1839, the bridge features the Burr construction style, with a curved truss support. Previous names have included Hummel's Bridge and Solt's Bridge, for a gristmill that once existed a hundred yards upstream.

THE HEX HIGHWAY
OLD ROUTE 22

THE ROUTE

Take Old Route 22 (the Hex Highway) west from Kuhnsville to Bethel.

There are basically two camps of thought when it comes to hex signs, the geometric folk art that Pennsylvania Dutch farmers painted on the sides of their barns. One camp believes each of the various symbols, such as the distelfink bird, eight-pointed star, and sheave of wheat, carries its own special meaning—perhaps an incantation against evil or a prayer for favorable spirits. The other camp is firmly convinced that the stylized paintings are simply designs borrowed from decorated documents like birth and marriage certificates to brighten the sides of the barns.

The one thing that both camps can agree on is that there is no better place to view hex signs in a wide variety of designs than Old Route 22—also known as the Hex Highway—in northern Berks County. Cruising from Kuhnsville west to Bethel, the traveler will pass several dozen barns adorned with the folk paintings. Many of the barns are more than a hundred years old.

In this agricultural region, still dominated by rolling hillsides of corn and grain, the "fancy" Pennsylvania Dutch—the colorful cousins of the more widely known "plain" Amish and Mennonites—settled generations ago. They were not averse to painting their furniture, household goods, and the like in bright, vibrant colors with designs they recalled from their ancestors in Germany.

Longevity is a way of life in this region, not only for the old farmers and farm wives, the barns, and the fields, but for businesses as well. Haag's Hotel in Shartlesville has served meals to travelers for more than one hundred years. Other enterprises may not have the century mark under their belts, but their wares certainly are authentic. The Deutsch Ech restaurant in Lenhartsville offers true Pennsylvania Dutch cooking accompanied by mint tea made from local wild varieties; Deitrich's Meats & Country Store in Krumsville is a real Pennsylvania Dutch butcher shop with delicacies like souse, jellied pig snout, and Lebanon bologna.

The Borough of Hamburg, with about eighteen hundred families living on five square miles along the Schuylkill River, is the largest community on this route. About a block south of Old Route 22 on Fourth Street stands one of the last true five-and-dimes in Pennsylvania. Miller's 5 & 10 (actually owned and operated by Mike and Lynn Heckart), doesn't carry much for a nickel or a dime, but it does stock what seems like a never-ending variety of items, from coin-collecting supplies to Christmas lights to furnace filters.

A block from Miller's, back on Old Route 22, stands the second reason for a pause in Hamburg. Inside the Adams & Bright Drug Store is a fully functioning soda fountain from decades ago, at which the proprietor still dispenses treats every Thursday and on special town celebration days. If you visit the store, don't miss the hundreds of antique pharmaceutical bottles—all in prime condition and containing varying amounts of their original contents—that line the walls behind the pharmacy counter. Last used sporadically to mix remedies like cough syrups in the late 1950s, the bottles have been dated to about 1900.

Shartlesville is the most touristy of the towns on this trip, with numerous craft and souvenir shops, a variety of dining opportunities, several buildings painted in bright pastels, and an attraction known as Roadside America. In an eight-thousand-square-foot, handmade, model-train-village display, the visitor is taken to scenes throughout the region, both modern and historical. Shartlesville is also home to the Fort Motel, which has combined a Fort Apache exterior motif, complete with log stockades, with a thousand-light display.

Country music fans will recognize the name of the next town on this route: Strausstown. The Pat Garrett Amphitheater attracts some of the biggest names in the business for open-air performances every summer. The country legend also operates an authentic roadhouse, with a karaoke night that can propel winners onto the amphitheater stage as opening acts.

Near the end of this route, just outside Bethel, lies the fifty-year-old Grimes Airfield, home of the Golden Age Air Museum, a constantly expanding collection of antique airplanes, equipment, and memorabilia housed in a growing array of hangars and other buildings.

Hex signs are painted on this barn near Kempton in Lehigh County.

ABOVE:

An Amish farmer cuts alfalfa in his field near Paradise in Lancaster County.

LEFT:

Amish farmers sterilize the soil by steaming it with a traction steam engine in preparation for planting.

WHAT DO HEX SIGNS MEAN?

The exact meaning, if any, for the symbols used in hex signs may be lost to antiquity.

Theories have developed and spread, particularly in the past few decades as hex signs became popular decoration well beyond the Pennsylvania Dutch community. A great many enthusiasts have interpreted the signs to symbolize the following: hearts for love, the distelfink bird for happiness, tulips for faith, stars for luck, shafts of wheat for abundance, and the sun wheel for fertility.

The bright colors used in painting the hex signs also have been ascribed certain properties, such as white for purity, blue for peace, green for fertility, red for passion, orange for abundance, violet for sacred objects, brown for strength, and yellow for health.

These hex signs come from a farm building in Intercourse.

BUCKS COUNTY
THE DELAWARE CANAL AND DELAWARE VALLEY

THE ROUTE

From Bristol, take U.S. Highway 13 north to Morrisville, Pennsylvania Highway 32 north to Kintnersville, then Pennsylvania Highway 611 north to Easton.

Workers began excavating the Delaware Division of the Pennsylvania Canal at Bristol in 1827. They completed the Bristol to New Hope section by 1830 and the entire Bristol to Easton run, where their canal linked with the Lehigh Navigation Canal, by 1832.

Those are important dates to the traveler on the following tour through Bucks County into Northampton County, because they help explain the early economic boost that communities along this route received, which propelled them to a status that continues to this day. Fortunes were made in the thirty-three million tons of coal that came down the canal system from Schuylkill and Carbon Counties. Businesses of all sorts grew to supply the workforce. Communities like Bristol, the start of our tour, expanded from rural villages to lively towns of more than a thousand. The boom trickled to an end by 1932, but the foundation had been laid for prosperous communities that have since found new directions.

Today, Delaware Canal State Park protects the sixty-mile length of the Delaware Canal, the only remaining continuously intact canal from the great towpath canal building era of the 1820s. Most features along the canal today remain as they were during that period of immense commercial expansion. The U.S. Congress added federal recognition in 1988, establishing the Delaware & Lehigh National Heritage Corridor along the same route.

Our route along Pennsylvania Highways 32 and 611 parallels the entire length of the Delaware Canal State Park, utilizing some of the many access points that have been created there. Opportunities for direct experiences with the canal and park are plentiful along our route, including taking mule-drawn barge rides at New Hope and Easton, hiking the towpath along the canal, and plying the waters by canoe, supplied by the numerous liveries along the shore.

The Delaware Valley, which comprises the southern half of this trip, is a historic region, rich with the events of early America. Remember, George Washington slept here—literally—and led the Continental Army that gave birth to a nation across this valley. But before we get to one of the most widely known of the Washington-related sites, Washington Crossing, there is much more to explore in some of the communities to the south.

Bristol was founded as Buckingham on a 262-acre land grant from the governor of New York to Samuel Clift in 1681, simultaneous with William Penn's charter from King Charles II of England. Among Clift's responsibilities was the founding of a ferry across the Delaware River and an inn at the ferry. His Ferry House, which has since been through a succession of names and is today called the King George II, is the oldest inn in continuous service in the United States. The traveler on this route can still have a meal and a tankard there, at 102 Radcliffe Street.

Levittown is of a much more recent historic vintage, but one of great importance to homeowners across the country. In this planned community—and in the Levitttowns of New York and New Jersey—after World War II, Abraham Levitt and his sons, Alfred and William, created and refined the concept of affordable, assembly-line homes. Builders could erect about two hundred of the homes each week—a good thing considering that thirty-five hundred were purchased in the first ten weeks of sales. The houses and the community were all tightly planned, with a washer, stove, and refrigerator included in the former and schools, places of worship, recreation areas, and shopping facilities set for the latter. Each new homeowner signed a purchase agreement binding him not to install fences around his property, change the color of his home, or hang laundry out on Sundays.

Farther north, we encounter Washington Crossing, one of the United States's most significant historic sites. Here, on Christmas night 1776, at what was then Delaware Crossing, General George Washington sent twenty-five hundred men of his Continental Army across the Delaware River and

WILLIAM PENN: PENNSYLVANIA'S FOUNDER

In 1681, the Quaker William Penn founded Pennsylvania, naming it Penns Woods for his father, Admiral Sir William Penn. He carved the new colony from a land grant given him by King Charles II of England in payment of a debt to the admiral. The colony was marked by a forward-thinking representative form of government and, while Penn was leading, fair and respectful treatment of the Native Americans who occupied the land.

A vintage Currier and Ives print depicts William Penn's treaty with the Indians when he founded the province of Pennsylvania.

Gray- and red-phase screech owls perch in a poppy field in western Lancaster County.

This lock keeper's house stands beside the Delaware Canal in New Hope.

ABOVE:
Tobacco dries in an Amish barn.

LEFT:
A lock is used to control the water flow of the Delaware Canal near Lumberville in Bucks County.

George Washington is immortalized in this classic Currier and Ives print, which portrays him crossing the Delaware before the Revolutionary War's famous battle at Trenton.

in the ensuing Battle of Trenton, in New Jersey, changed the tide of the Revolutionary War. Believing the Americans to be too weak to attack Trenton, British General William Howe sent most of his soldiers to New York and Newport. The British and Hessians left in Trenton were in a Christmas mood—relaxed, drunk, and unsuspecting of an attack. The American victory, which took a thousand prisoners in an hour and captured Trenton, gave Washington's army hope for the first time that winter. If they had lost this battle, the Americans could have lost the War for Independence.

Washington Crossing Historic Park was founded in 1917 to preserve the site, which includes a collection of old taverns, inns, homes, and mills. More recently it has come to include the one-hundred-acre Bowman's Hill Wildflower Preserve, a collection of more than a thousand species of Pennsylvania native plants in a naturalistic setting, traversed by more than two dozen trails.

New Hope, farther north, is the sophisticated yet country-casual gem of the regional art scene. More than two hundred art galleries, antique shops, boutiques, and one-of-a-kind craft and specialty shops line its quaint streets. Everything from a gourmet picnic along the canal to lunch at an outdoor café to continental cuisine at a country inn can be had in New Hope. The community has also developed as a haven for modern musicians, artists, and writers.

Easton, the northern terminus of our tour, is packed with places of historical interest. Directly related to the Delaware Canal is Two Rivers Landing, with the Delaware and Lehigh National Heritage Corridor Visitor Center on the first floor and the National Canal Museum on the third floor, which holds exhibits about the history and technology of the nineteenth-century canals and inland waterway system. Hugh Moore Park in the city is home to an 1890s locktender's house that has been made into a canal museum.

Easton is also home to Binney & Smith, the company that produces the boxes of Crayola crayons for the desks of every child in America. Founded in 1864 by Joseph Binney as Peekskill Chemical Works in upstate New York, the company first manufactured charcoal and lamp black. In 1885, Binney retired and his son, Edwin, formed a partnership with C. Harold Smith. Early products of Binney & Smith were red oxide pigment for barn paint and carbon black for car tires. The company moved to Easton in 1902, noticed a need for safe and affordable wax crayons, and began producing the first boxes of eight—red, orange, yellow, green, blue, violet, brown, and black—which were sold for a nickel. Take time to tour the factory and visit the interactive museum.

FOR THE BIRDS
MIDDLE CREEK WILDLIFE MANAGEMENT AREA

Middle Creek Wildlife Management Area, a six-thousand-acre tract of wetlands, fields, and woodlands in Lebanon and Lancaster Counties, is one of the premier birding spots in the state. Waterfowl are the stars, but dozens of songbird and raptor species are also spotted regularly at the site. Since its creation in the 1970s, the area has become the year-round home to an incredible array of wildlife and is a major stopover for migrating birds along the Atlantic Flyway each spring and fall. Middle Creek's appeal to waterfowl lies in the diversity of preferred habitats the birds find at the site. This diversity is a direct result of wildlife plantings, habitat enhancements, and wetland creation and manipulation.

For travelers hoping to witness certain species of birds at Middle Creek, it's a matter of timing. Snow geese are late-winter visitors. In the early 1990s only small numbers came to Middle Creek. Then, in 1997, a phenomenal 150,000 blanketed the site's fields and lake. The birds have been visiting in large numbers ever since on their migration north to the eastern arctic region. The total Atlantic Flyway population of snow geese is approximately 700,000.

Tundra swans have been late-winter and early spring visitors for decades, and in the past several years have started to winter at Middle Creek. Their occupation of the area tends to parallel that of the snow geese. They visited in small numbers until 1997, when an unexpected eight thousand settled in to prepare for the flight north. In 2001, the Middle Creek number climbed to fourteen thousand swans.

Numbers of Canada geese and many duck species swell with the spring and fall migrations, although large numbers of the honkers and ducks are residents of the site. A wide variety of black ducks, mallards, and shovelers regularly cruise the impoundments. The many broods of young Canada geese trailing their mothers are an attraction in early summer.

THE ROUTE

From Kleinfeltersville, drive south on Hopeland Road. Take Township Road 307 east to Pin Tail Drive, and that road southeast to Township Road 638. Move southeast to Township Road 650, and then south to Furnace Hill Road. Travel east to Girl Scout Road and then south to Township Road 987. Go west to Millstone Road and then south to Kleinfeltersville Road. Take Kleinfeltersville Road north to Museum Road and that west to the visitor center parking lot. From there, go east on Museum Road and north on Kleinfeltersville Road to Hopeland Road, which runs north to Kleinfeltersville.

OVERLEAF:

A foggy summer morning surrounds wheat shocks on an Amish farm near Leola.

In addition to the waterfowl, several showy species of raptors are active at Middle Creek. Northern harriers, or marsh hawks, patrol the fields. A pair of bald eagles lives and has successfully nested along the southern and eastern shores of the lake. Songbirds, too, are abundant residents in the varied habitats initially developed for waterfowl. Middle Creek is now a major bluebird nesting area, with an actively managed trail of nestboxes. And, it's been a rare visit to the site when I've not spotted at least a few red fox and many white-tailed deer, including bucks with impressive antlers in season.

The Pennsylvania Game Commission, which operates Middle Creek—largely with money from the sale of hunting licenses—closes some of the interior roadways to public traffic during winter and spring. This gives the waterfowl a respite, but it also eliminates access to some of the most intimate and close-up views of the four-hundred-acre lake, many small impoundments, wetlands, and birds. Keep this in mind when you visit the area.

Time of day is also an important consideration for the traveler. Seeing some wildlife at Middle Creek can be accomplished at any time, but early morning and late afternoon or early evening are prime for maximizing potential sightings, as those are the times when wildlife are most active. Geese, for example, leave the lake and ponds to feed in nearby fields at sunrise. They reverse that route, converging by the thousands on the main lake, at sunset.

Much of our route through Middle Creek follows the well-signed self-guided driving tour, which carries the visitor close to many points of interest. Included along the route are the Waterfowl Habitat View, a dozen dikes (planted with millet in June each year and then flooded in the fall to provide feeding areas for waterfowl), four picnic areas, and a boating access area on the lake. The visitor center, just off Hopeland Road near the western shore of the lake, houses a large wildlife exhibit, including an extensive display of taxidermist-mounted waterfowl and a separate display of the nests and eggs of various bird species.

A pair of binoculars or a spotting scope is helpful on this route. Although there are numerous opportunities to drive within a few yards of the wildlife, binoculars or a scope will ensure up-close looks at the critters.

This is also a great tour to pause, park the vehicle, stroll a bit on the site's nine miles of developed trails, and get a first-hand look at the Middle Creek area. Willow Point Trail, for example, is an easy walk to an entirely different vantage point over the main lake.

DUTCH COUNTRY
THE AMISH OF LANCASTER COUNTY

Lancaster County is one of the most ironic places on Earth. The Amish, the original settlers of the region, shun modern ways and conveniences to enjoy a peaceful, agrarian lifestyle. But in their nonelectric, nonmotorized world, they have created the foundation for a thriving tourist industry, parts of which relate directly to them and parts of which are far removed from their pastoral farms.

Just about any road through Lancaster County will carry the traveler on this cultural roller coaster, as the most modern of businesses and buildings intermingle with the one-room schoolhouses, windwheels, and horse-drawn buggies of the "Plain People." Pennsylvania Highways 23 and 340, however, offer the optimum blend of close-up glimpses at the everyday farms and homes of the Amish and a diverse array of topnotch tourist attractions and eateries. Be prepared for culture shock as you first pass a small country church with several dozen horse-drawn buggies tied in the stables outside, then a mall of specialty stores, then a farmer working his fields with benefit of only mule power, then the finely decorated exterior of an upscale restaurant.

THE ROUTE

From Morgantown, take Pennsylvania Highway 23 west to Lancaster, then Pennsylvania Highway 340 east to White Horse.

To list all of the hundreds of attractions along this route would be impossible here, but there are standouts that provide a taste of the essence of this region. An on-road buggy ride, such as that provided by Abe's Buggy Rides in Bird-in-Hand, allows the tourist to experience, in a small way, the rigors of horse-drawn transportation amid the modern flow of motorized traffic. The Amish Country Homestead, also in Bird-in-Hand, provides a sanitized but mostly accurate look inside a typical Amish home and

farm. The People's Place Quilt Museum in Intercourse offers a contemplative study of the craftsmanship that goes into everything produced by these unobtrusive people. The Bird-in-Hand Farmers Market, and several similar markets along the route, spreads out the special foods of the region in booth after booth.

The rich farmland of southeastern Pennsylvania allows for several wineries. These wine casks advertise the Mount Hope Wine Gallery in Intercourse.

The sun sets over a January snowfall near White Horse in Lancaster County.

LEFT:

An eastern box turtle wanders through a patch of wild pansies in Lancaster County.

FAR LEFT:
Tracks run through a frozen stream in Chester County.

LEFT:
Purple Dead Nettle grow in a field along Silver Springs Road near Holtwood.

A whitetail yearling gives its mother a lick.

A touch of the Dutch influence even carries over into the non-Amish attractions. The thirty-two shops of the Kitchen Kettle Village in Intercourse offer much Amish-style merchandise but also show the influence of the modern mall. Some other parts of Lancaster are much more populated by outlet malls, but this route does offer some highly specialized operations, like the Home Furnishings Outlet Mall in Morgantown (the largest of its kind in the state) and the Good Food Outlet Store in Leola.

When the Pennsylvania Dutch Country Welcome Center surveys repeat visitors, the number one reason they give for returning to the region is the food. Pennsylvania Dutch cooking—large portions of rich, heavy, and sweet fare—is the local cuisine, often served smorgasbord-style. However, just about any taste and price range can be accommodated along this route.

The Pennsylvania Dutch influence naturally continues into the small city of Lancaster, but it quickly blends with a considerably more urbane and artsy atmosphere. The city was the largest inland town in the United States from the 1760s to the early 1800s and even served as the nation's capital for one day in September 1777. Today, it continues to have a truly aristocratic air. Built in 1852, Lancaster's Fulton Opera House is America's oldest continuously operating theater. The Central Market is reminiscent of the inner-city open-air markets of butchers, bakers, farmers, and other purveyors seen in much larger metropolitan areas.

RIVERBANK CULTURE
THE LOWER SUSQUEHANNA RIVER

THE ROUTE

Beginning in Peach Bottom, motor west on Paper Mill Road (State Route 2024), north on McKinley Road, northeast on Slab Road, northwest on River Road, and east on Pennsylvania Highway 372 across the Susquehanna River. Head northwest on Pinnacle Road through Holtwood and Tucquan, then drive southeast on River Road, south on State Road 3017, east on Highway 372, south on State Road 3009, and west and south on River Road to Susquehannock State Park.

Small towns and villages along a river seem to be carved from a different culture than communities of similar sizes away from the riverine setting. Although conditions are changing quickly as new money buys out original riverbank families to construct new high-end homes, river towns have often seemed to follow a slower pace. Perhaps the residents are more in step with the seasons of the water flowing nearby, with less concern over the tidiness of the front lawn than the demands and opportunities on the water. There's a boat in every backyard and, if at all possible, a dock or pebbly beach down at the river. Pockets along the lower Susquehanna River, through which the traveler will pass on this route, exhibit both the old culture of local residents and the influence of outside wealth moving into the communities.

The section of the Susquehanna River we follow here is nearing the end of its 444-mile run from Cooperstown, New York, to the Chesapeake Bay at Havre de Grace, Maryland. The nation's sixteenth-largest river is also at its widest and most island-strewn in this area. More than sixty islands are scattered throughout this stretch of the river, known collectively as the Conowingo Islands. Upper and Lower Bear Islands, the largest two of the chain, can be seen downriver from the Pennsylvania Highway 372 bridge, which stands at about the midpoint of our tour. Some of the islands contain virgin stands of beech and hemlocks.

Upriver from the bridge, the traveler can spot the Holtwood Hydroelectric Dam, one of several massive barriers stretched across the river in this area to harness the power of the Susquehanna. Also in this area is the Peach Bottom site, where we begin our drive. Philadelphia Electric Company, a pioneer in the U.S. nuclear industry, employed an experimental gas-cooled reactor at Peach Bottom Unit I as early as the late 1950s.

Most lands surrounding the dams and power plants have been developed into various public recreation facilities by the utilities that own them. Muddy Run Park is the most developed of these sites, with camping, boating, and fishing on a lake developed as pumped-storage capacity for the utility. A large and visible deer herd is also resident here.

Those dams brought about the temporary end to the annual shad migration up the Susquehanna River, which in the late 1800s supported an entire industry of seine fisheries and provided untold and badly needed food stores for countless residents along the river. Shad were completely cut off from their ancestral spawning grounds by the construction of four large hydro-dams—one each at York Haven, Safe Harbor, and Holtwood in Pennsylvania, and Conowingo in Maryland—between 1904 and 1932.

Long-awaited restoration efforts began in 1991, when Philadelphia Electric Company built a fish-lift capable of carrying 750,000 adult shad over Conowingo Dam each year. Since then, in the largest effort of its kind in the nation, passages have been installed at the other three hydro-dams upriver from Conowingo. Today, tens of thousands of shad are again making the breeding run.

At the northernmost apex of our route, north of the village of Holtwood, the Lancaster County Conservancy has created the Tucquan Glen Nature Preserve. Included in the preserve is the Pyfer Nature Preserve, the premier natural area in southeastern Pennsylvania and the most pristine of the seven ravines or glens which open into the Susquehanna River here. In April and May, at least three dozen common wildflowers, such as trilliums, can be seen along the trail and hillsides. In addition, two dozen species of ferns can be found, including three uncommon species. The forest canopy is spectacular, and many trees reach eighty feet or more.

Susquehannock State Park, with its river and island vistas from atop 380-foot cliffs, concludes this tour. Among the islands clearly visible from the overlook is Mt. Johnson Island—the first bald eagle sanctuary in the United States—as well as other sites being used today by nesting eagles. The 224-acre park offers a variety of recreational opportunities, including picnicking and hiking. A system of trails winds its way among old homestead sites, such as the former Landis House, built in 1850.

PART V

RIVERS AND RIVER VALLEYS: SOUTH-CENTRAL PENNSYLVANIA

FACING PAGE:

This weathered, white barn in Franklin County sports five cupolas.

ABOVE:

At the end of an Amish farm lane, milk cans wait to be picked up and taken to local co-op.

The fortunes of the south-central part of Pennsylvania rise and fall with new developments in transportation. This has been true for centuries. The Iroquois increased their worth and strength with raids on other Native American tribes to the south by using timeworn trails through this region. Early European settlement followed those same trails, expanding them into wagon roads, and then boomed with the coming of the railroads. Later, south-central Pennsylvania introduced the first named coast-to-coast highway.

Important parts of the nation's history were written on the lands of this region. Battles between European settlers and Native Americans, then battles between those European settlers and their former countrymen, and, finally, battles between the northern and southern descendents of those European settlers were fought here.

The region is crossed by an abundance of large to mid-size waterways, from wide rivers like the Susquehanna to large streams like the Yellow Breeches, which also played their part in the development of the area's cultural character. They all continue to function as substantial providers to the increasingly important recreational economy.

With a few exceptions, cities in the south-central region are small, towns are spaced by long expanses of forest, and villages often haven't changed much for many years. Numerous riverside communities have a main street set back a block or two from the water and provide ready access to the water, often in the form of parks and ramps for launching boats.

THE ROUTE

From Benvenue, take Pennsylvania Highway 849 north, then Aqueduct Road northeast, to Lower Bailey Road. Follow that north and west to Newport. From there take Highway 849 north, Old Ferry Road north, Detour Road northeast, and State Route 4006 northwest to Millerstown. Drive west on U.S. Highway 22/322 to Thompsontown, then follow Pennsylvania Highway 333 south and west to Port Royal. Take Highway 333 north, Pennsylvania Highway 103 west and south to Mt. Union, and U.S. Highway 22 north then west to Huntingdon.

CHASING THE RIVER
THE JUNIATA RIVER VALLEY

The Juniata River just might be the most beautiful river in Pennsylvania, particularly when seen from the wilder western shore. While the eastern shore is more highly developed, most towns on the west side of the river have remained small and retained substantial parts of their character from decades past. Farmers have cut fields into the rich soil, and tracks of the Pennsylvania Railroad do follow the curves of the river, but vast stretches of land along the western shore remain in a natural state.

The Juniata is a shallow, slow-moving, meandering river with a rocky bottom, packed with small islands and extensive areas of flats. It's a prime ecosystem for wading birds and waterfowl, although birders have recorded more than 150 species of birds along the river. The typical array of mammal life, from white-tailed deer to chipmunks, is abundant; water-loving species like mink and beaver are common; and river otter have been reintroduced by the Pennsylvania Game Commission. The plant community is diverse, as the zone around the river varies from floodplains to hillsides to steep cliffs.

ALTOONA

LEWISTOWN

TUSCARORA
THOMPSONTOWN

26

HUNTINGDON

PORT ROYAL

MILLERSTOWN

22

333

22

NEWPORT

103

Juniata River

NEW BLOOMFIELD

BENVENUE

Raystown Lake

GREEN PARK

26

MT. UNION

233

34

FREDERICKSBURG

DOUBLING GAP

CARLISLE

36

NEWVILLE

Kings Gap

WARRIORS PATH
STATE PARK

SAXTON

15

NEWBURG

641

MONTSERA

*Raystown Branch
Juniata River*

696

76

SHIPPENSBURG

WALNUT
BOTTOM

HUNTERS RUN

174

PINE GROVE FURNACE

PINE GROVE
FURNACE
STATE PARK

BEDFORD

MICHAUX
STATE FOREST

233

FLORADALE

EVERETT

BREEZEWOOD

CHAMBERSBURG

34

MCCONNELLSBURG

30

30

FORT LOUDON

CALEDONIA

NEW OXFORD

70

81

*Gettysburg National
Military Park*

GETTYSBURG

*Susquehanna
River*

Cumulus clouds collect over an autumn farm scene in Huntingdon County.

Humans have used the Juniata River, and the flat river lowlands along much of it, as transportation for thousands of years. Prehistoric native peoples used it, and today U.S. Highway 22/322, on the opposite side of the river from most of our route, is a primary roadway through a substantial portion of the middle of the state. The railroad line the traveler along this route encounters frequently was built by the Pennsylvania Railroad in 1849. Traces of the long-abandoned Great Canal, Pennsylvania's answer to New York's Erie Canal, can also be seen along the river.

Even the name of the river has overtones of travel. *Juniata,* a Native American word from the Andaste people, means "standing stone" and refers to a projecting rock at the point that Standing Stone Creek empties into the Juniata River in Huntingdon. Perhaps that rock once served as a landmark in the travel directions of native residents.

Although historically humans have passed through this region rather than stopped to develop it, some large towns have grown here, such as Newport, Lewistown, and Huntingdon. A unique event in the Lewistown area of the Juniata Valley warrants special mention: It is one of the few places to celebrate Goose Day every September 29. Organizations here have taken to heart a centuries-old English proverb that advises, "Eat goose on Michaelmas Day and you will never want for money all the year round." The Chamber of Commerce hosts a Goose Day luncheon. One out-of-state motorist is stopped and invited to join in the feast of roast goose, after which he or she is presented with a crate of specialty products from the region and sent on his or her way. Many local restaurants and volunteer fire companies hold roast goose dinners. And, the weekends around September 29 are filled with harvest festivals, craft shows, horse shows, and the Wild Goose Chase road rally.

BETWEEN THE SUSQUEHANNA AND THE SHENANDOAH
THE CUMBERLAND VALLEY

THE ROUTE

Starting in Carlisle, drive south on Pennsylvania Highway 34 and west on Pennsylvania Highway 174 to Shippensburg. From there, motor north on Pennsylvania Highway 696, east on Pennsylvania Highway 641 at Newburg, north on Pennsylvania Highway 233 at Newville, east on Pennsylvania Highway 274 at Green Park, and south on Highway 34 to Carlisle.

The Cumberland Valley is a broad plain—at places twenty-five miles across—stretching from the Susquehanna River to the Shenandoah River. Much of this route carries the traveler right down the middle of the valley at one of its widest spots. There, towering North Mountain rises like a wall, while the gently sloping South Mountain climbs at a slower pace, but both reach elevations of seven hundred to twelve hundred feet above the valley floor.

The valley was the farthest inland reach of civilization in the late 1700s. It drew farmers with its rich soil and foundrymen with its iron-rich limestone and plentiful supply of trees for charcoal. After its frontier days, the relative ease of travel through the valley made it a primary thoroughfare for settlement farther west.

The natural highway from Virginia into the North that was, and is, the Cumberland Valley wasn't lost on Confederate tacticians in the Civil War. The valley was raided repeatedly by parties looking for supplies to take back to the South. And, in June 1863, General Robert E. Lee swung his force of seventy-five thousand north through the valley, capturing Carlisle and failing to take Harrisburg only after the bridge at Wrightsville was burned to stop his advance. Those events transpired in the days immediately preceding the critical Battle of Gettysburg on July 1–3, 1863.

Carlisle had a varied history both before and after the Civil War. Founded in 1751, the town was George Washington's choice for his army's first arsenal and military school. It was also home to the nation's first school for Native Americans. The Carlisle Indian School operated from 1879 to 1918. Today, the town is home to the U.S. Army War College, as well as the Military History Institute with its Omar N. Bradley Museum and the Hessian Powder Magazine Museum.

Just outside the town, the eighty-two-acre fairgrounds is the site of the Carlisle Collector Car Swap Meet and Corral—the largest show of its kind—as well as several other car, truck, and motorcycle shows throughout the year. Auto enthusiasts from around the world attend the big show, which features about eighty-one hundred vendors and fifteen hundred car corral spaces.

Shippensburg, founded in 1730 when a dozen Scotch-Irish families erected cabins along Burd's Run, is the oldest community of the Cumberland Valley and the second-oldest Pennsylvania community west of the Susquehanna River. It was named for Edward Shippen, a prominent resident of Lancaster who obtained the patent to the land from heirs of William Penn. The town, home to seventy-two-hundred-student Shippensburg University, the Community Fair each July, and the Corn Festival arts and crafts street fair each August, was rated number twenty-seven by Norman Crampton in his 1995 book, *100 Best Small Towns in America*.

The former Stewart House, built in 1784, houses the museum of the Shippensburg Historical Society, which includes one of the largest collections of artifacts from the Works Progress Administration. The WPA was the largest and most important of the New Deal cultural programs, a massive employment relief program launched in the spring of 1935 by the Roosevelt administration.

In Newville, more treasures can be found. Although only the John McCullough House just southeast of town and the Sterreitt-Hassinger House in the center of town are on the National Register of Historic Places, the village is packed with prime examples of historic architectural styles, many well maintained.

Just outside Newville, a World War I reenactment is held biannually on forty acres cut with trenches, dugouts, and authentic obstacles to recreate the feel of the Western Front.

ABOVE:

The Laughlin Grist Mill of Newville was built in 1763 by William Laughlin and is the oldest structure in the region.

LEFT:

This hand pump remains next to the Olive Branch School, a one-room schoolhouse in Tuscarora.

FACING PAGE, TOP:

Lewistown Station, on Highway 103 in Mifflin County, is the oldest remaining structure built by the Pennsylvania Railroad.

FACING PAGE, BOTTOM:

Apple trees blossom near Arendtsville in Adams County.

A bit north of town, the magnitude of the Cumberland Valley at its widest can be seen from Pennsylvania Highway 233 as the road climbs North Mountain at Doubling Gap. The gap was thus named because the mountain doubles over to an "M," creating two valley passes immediately next to one another.

The heart of the valley is famous for world-class trout fishing. Stream names instantly recognizable to any trout angler abound in the Cumberland Valley. Anglers worldwide have made the trip to fish in these waters, and our tour crosses several streams. The Letort, most famous of all Pennsylvania trout streams, runs under Pennsylvania Highway 34 just south of Carlisle; the Yellow Breeches, one of the most popular trout streams in the state, flows under Pennsylvania Highway 174 east of Walnut Bottom; and Big Spring Creek flows through Newville.

PLATEAUS OF PENNSYLVANIA
THE MICHAUX STATE FOREST REGION

THE ROUTE

Take Kings Gap Road south from Montsera to Kings Gap Environmental Education Center. From there, again take Kings Gap Road south, Ridge Road east, Pennsylvania Highway 34 south, Hunters Run Road southwest, and State Route 3008 southwest to Pine Grove Furnace. Follow Pennsylvania Highway 233 southwest, Woodrow Road north, Ridge Road southwest, and Three Turn Road north then west. Follow Thompson Hollow Road south, Ridge Road west, Pennsylvania Highway 997 southeast, and Pennsylvania Highway 30 east through Caledonia. Take Piney Mountain Ridge Road northeast, Millenberger Road south, Berger Road south, Buchannan Valley Road east, Narrows Road east, State Route 4008 north, then State Route 4004 east to Floradale.

The South Mountains of the Michaux area rise in a gradual, rolling fashion from the Cumberland Valley to the north then top out in broad, flat plateaus. This gives each plateau and each stream-carved hollow slanting down off the plateau a feeling of vastness.

Incorporating large portions of the mountainscape is the eighty-five-thousand-acre Michaux State Forest, named for Andre Michaux, a French botanist dispatched by the King and Queen of France in 1785 to search American forests for new species of trees that might be planted to rebuild the forests of France. After almost a century of war with England, French forests had been stripped of the best trees to construct a never-ending stream of warships. Michaux and his son, Francois Andre Michaux, are remembered for discovering and identifying hundreds of trees, shrubs, and wildflowers.

When Michaux visited America, large iron companies owned the forest area that would later bear his name. Immense iron furnaces at Caledonia and Pine Grove Furnace processed iron ore, dug from open pits, into pig iron, the raw material that was then forged into tools, kettles, and other implements. Wood cut from the vast mountainous tract was converted through carefully controlled burns over ten to fourteen days into charcoal, which was used to fuel the iron furnaces. Remains of the large hearths that the colliers used in the process can be seen in many spots of the Michaux. They are dry circles free of vegetation, about thirty-five to fifty feet in diameter. Bits of charcoal can still be found amid the forest litter at these sites.

As the charcoal industry began to decline in the early 1900s, James McCormick Cameron bought considerable acreage in the Michaux to locate a summerhouse outside the family's home city of Harrisburg. The thirty-two-room stone mansion he had built in 1908 of native Antietam quartzite quarried from a nearby ridge is today the main facility of the

Kings Gap Environmental Education and Training Center, part of Pennsylvania's state park system. The mansion also serves as the William C. Forrey Training Center for the state, providing meals and overnight lodging for government agencies, and is used for various environmental education programs for the public.

Most of the 1,454 acres of Kings Gap are open for public use. The site is crossed by 16 miles of trails, including the 1.9-mile Rock Scree Trail, which leads hikers past the ridge where the mansion stone was quarried to a magnificent view of the Cumberland Valley. Several spots at Kings Gap, including the stone veranda of the mansion, offer similarly panoramic views of the wide valley.

Pine Grove Furnace State Park occupies the site of one of the region's eighteenth-century iron furnaces. The ironmaster's mansion, a gristmill, an inn, and several workers' residences are still maintained, and a 1.25-mile self-guided historic trail leads through the site. In addition, the state park holds the midpoint of the Appalachian Trail, a spot where through-hikers traditionally down a quart of ice cream in celebration of putting more than a thousand miles behind them. From this spot it's roughly 1,050 miles to each end of the trail—Mt. Katahdin in central Maine to the north and Springer Mountain in Georgia to the south.

Our route through the Michaux State Forest also takes us past several historic fire watchtowers. We will see the site of the first forest fire tower, a wooden structure built in 1905; the site of the first steel fire tower, built in 1914; and the only site where vandals cut down a steel fire tower, in 1972.

THE POLITICAL CAMERON FAMILY

James McCormick Cameron, the man who built the mountaintop mansion that is today the Kings Gap Environmental Education and Training Center, was part of the politically prominent Cameron family of Harrisburg.

His grandfather, Simon Cameron, served as a U.S. senator for Pennsylvania and, for a brief period, Secretary of War under Abraham Lincoln during the Civil War. His father, James Donald Cameron, was also a U.S. senator for the Keystone State. Both men amassed fortunes through banking, steel mills, printing, and railroading.

James McCormick Cameron built upon the fortunes he inherited, but—hampered by a hearing problem that left him shy and soft-spoken—never took an interest in politics. What he did do was amass twenty-seven hundred acres in the Michaux region on which he instituted stewardship practices to protect the land.

REMEMBERING THE CIVIL WAR
GETTYSBURG NATIONAL MILITARY PARK

Gettysburg National Military Park covers six thousand acres, with twenty-six miles of park roads and more than fourteen hundred monuments, markers, and memorials. Historians at the National Park Service have designed an eighteen-mile self-guided auto tour across the park that would be difficult to improve. The full tour, in sixteen stops, covers much of what took place July 1–3, 1863, in the Battle of Gettysburg. Nothing compares to standing on the site and reading about what took place there for truly feeling history.

The three-day battle was the largest and bloodiest of the Civil War, resulting in more than 51,000 soldiers killed, wounded, or captured (about 23,000 Union and 28,000 Confederate). A little more than 82,000 Union troops started the battle against approximately 75,000 Confederate forces.

THE ROUTE

Beginning at the Gettysburg National Military Park's visitor center, follow the marked signs through the auto tour route.

FACING PAGE AND RIGHT:
The Battle of Gettysburg comes to life in this re-enactment at Gettysburg National Military Park.

BELOW:
The Pennsylvania Cavalry Monument stands as a memorial to fallen soldiers.

TRACING THE BATTLE

The National Park Service has developed an eighteen-mile auto tour that begins at the visitor center and traces the three-day Battle of Gettysburg, most in a chronological succession. The tour takes about three hours to fully appreciate and includes the following highlights.

• Stop 1, McPherson Ridge. The battle began at 8 A.M., July 1, 1863, just west of the McPherson barn, when Union cavalry confronted Confederate infantry. As additional forces from both armies joined in, the fighting spread north and south along the ridge.

• Stop 2, Eternal Light Peace Memorial on Barlow Knoll. Confederate forces under Major General Robert E. Rodes attack the Union positions along McPherson Ridge from this hill at 1 P.M., July 1. General Jubal Early's Confederates smashed the Union line here at 3 P.M.

• Stop 3, Oak Ridge. Union soldiers held out here until 3:30 P.M., July 1 against the Confederate attack.

• Stop 4, North Carolina Memorial, Seminary Ridge. Early on July 2 the Confederate army positioned itself on the high ground along this ridge, through the town of Gettysburg, and north of Cemetery and Culp's Hills, while Union forces occupied the two hills and Cemetery Ridge, south to the Round Tops.

• Stop 5, Virginia Memorial. The famous Pickett's Charge, last Confederate assault of the battle, took place in these fields on July 3.

• Stop 6, Pitzer Woods. Lieutenant General James Longstreet anchored the left of his Confederate line in these woods in the afternoon of July 2.

• Stop 7, Warfield Ridge. Here, Longstreet's forces began assaults at 4 P.M., July 2 against Union troops at Devil's Den, the Wheatfield, the Peach Orchard, and the Round Tops.

• Stop 8, Little Round Top. Only quick action by Brigadier General Gouvernour K. Warren, chief engineer of Union General George Meade, prevented Confederate forces from taking this strategic location on July 2.

• Stop 9, the Wheatfield. More than four thousand dead and wounded soldiers from both armies were left on this field after charge and countercharge on July 2.

• Stop 10, the Peach Orchard. Union cannons bombarded Confederate forces from here throughout the day on July 2, until Confederate soldiers finally overran the position.

• Stop 11, Plum Run. Union soldiers retreating from the Peach Orchard plunged through this small stream on their way to Cemetery Ridge.

• Stop 12, Pennsylvania Memorial, Cemetery Ridge. Union artillery held this ground under heavy Confederate assault, until reinforcements could be pulled from other parts of the battlefield on July 2.

• Stop 13, Spangler's Spring. Confederates captured and occupied this position at 7 P.M. July 2, only to be driven back by Union forces after seven hours of intense fighting the next day.

• Stop 14, East Cemetery Hill. As the sun was setting July 2, charging Confederate forces reached the crest of this hill before being repelled by Union soldiers.

• Stop 15, High Water Mark. In the climactic moment of the battle, seven thousand Union soldiers around the Copse of Trees, the Angle, and the Brian Barn repulsed the bulk of the twelve-thousand-man Pickett's Charge. The Confederate army began retreating.

• Stop 16, National Cemetery. This was the site of President Abraham Lincoln's Gettysburg Address on November 19, 1863.

The stage was set for the battle on Tuesday morning, June 30, when a Confederate infantry brigade moving toward Gettysburg in search of shoes and other supplies spotted a column of Union cavalry also moving toward the town and withdrew. The next morning, two divisions of Confederates moved back toward Gettysburg and encountered the Union cavalry west of town at Willoughby Run. The first skirmish began and then escalated as both armies rushed men, horses, and artillery to the scene.

The Battle of Gettysburg was the turning point in the war, resulting in the retreat of the second and final invasion of the North by General Robert E. Lee's Army of Northern Virginia. Historians often refer to it as the "High Water Mark of the Confederacy."

In addition to the battlefield tour, the town of Gettysburg itself is as packed building-to-building with museums and historic sites as any community in Pennsylvania.

The long and bloody Battle of Gettysburg began on July 1, 1863, and ended on July 3. Here, a print by Currier and Ives illustrates the violence of the rout.

THE LINCOLN HIGHWAY
U.S. HIGHWAY 30

Roads in the United States of 1912 were ruts that led pretty much nowhere other than the nearest town or the surrounding countryside. They were bumpy beyond modern imagination, and in wet weather they became swampy quagmires. The train was a much easier means to reach your destination.

THE ROUTE

From New Oxford, follow U.S. Highway 30 west to Bedford.

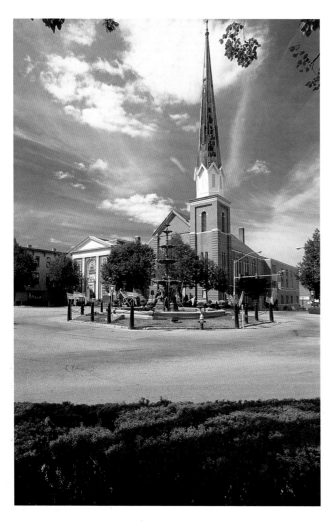

Chambersburg is rich with historic architecture. Pictured here is the town's center square.

There is more than one way to travel the backroads of the Keystone State. These custom Harley-Davidson motorcycles park for a break on their way through south-central Pennsylvania.

A newly mown hayfield stretches out to the horizon south of Carlisle in Cumberland County.

Carl Fisher, one of the founders of the Indianapolis Motor Speedway, had pondered road conditions for some time when he arrived at the concept of a coast-to-coast highway, topped with gravel, that ran all the way from New York City to San Francisco. A number of schemes were hatched to raise the ten million dollars that Fisher estimated the roadway would cost, including the naming of the highway for Abraham Lincoln in the hopes to play on the emotions of the American people.

The project progressed a bit, but not without substantial squabbling among factions wanting the first transcontinental highway to run through their state. It was eventually decided the route would make a nearly straight run across the country, starting at Times Square in New York; passing through New Jersey, Pennsylvania, Ohio, Indiana, Illinois, Iowa, Nebraska, Wyoming, Utah, and Nevada; and ending in San Francisco's Lincoln Park.

The United States soon progressed from one named highway in 1915 to an unorganized and confusing mess of them by 1925. The various highways marked their routes by painting colored bands on telephone poles. At points where several named highways shared the same route, the entire pole was covered like a rainbow. The confusion led to our current system of officially numbered highways, although the Lincoln Highway has held onto its identity.

The Lincoln Highway Association closed up shop in 1927, the year the highway was completed. For its last major activity, the association enlisted Boy Scouts to place small, concrete name markers at each mile along the highway.

New Oxford stands at the beginning of our Lincoln Highway drive. Dubbed "The Little Town with the Beautiful Circle," it is exactly what that slogan implies. The small village of vintage eighteenth- and nineteenth-century architecture surrounds a broad, grassy, town-center circle. Our route enters and exits the circle, passing by several fine restaurants and a selection of antique shops. Until after the Civil War, the town was home to the New Oxford College and Medical Institute, founded in 1864 by Dr. M. D. G. Pfeiffer.

Chambersburg is another beautiful community packed with historic architecture. Most of the older buildings, however, were built of necessity in the post–Civil War period. On July 30, 1864, after residents of the town refused to pay a one-hundred-thousand-dollar ransom to Confederate General John McCausland, he ordered his troops to torch the town. More than five hundred buildings were destroyed in this only act of town burning in the North.

A rebuilt and much grown Chambersburg celebrates its rebirth in mid July each year with ChambersFest, a day-long street festival of arts, crafts, food, pet parade, Almost Anything Goes Games, and Summer Jam youth event. A special feature of ChambersFest is the Civil War Seminar and Tour, which has attracted top Civil War authorities like Edwin Bearrs, Dennis Frye, Perry Jamieson, Stephen Oates, and Jeffery Wert.

Chambersburg has a long connection with the events of the Civil War. Beginning in 1859, anti-slavery zealot John Brown planned his raid on Harpers Ferry in a rented room at 225 East King Street. Confederate troops under General J. E. B. Stuart pillaged and raided Chambersburg railroad warehouses and local stores in 1862. The decision to move to Gettysburg was made by Confederate Generals Robert E. Lee and A. P. Hill at Memorial Diamond, the center of town.

Fort Loudon's mark on history extends to an earlier period, when the primary worry for residents and travelers was the Native Americans. One of the many forts the British erected to protect travel in their colonies, Fort Loudon was built in 1756. It was the first British fort ever taken by colonial Americans. On March 9, 1765, three hundred Americans led by James Smith rousted the King's men from the fort.

McConnellsburg came into being in the 1760s, when a collection of houses grew up around a stopping place on the main wagon route to the West from Philadelphia. The historic district of the town has 144 buildings in styles that include Georgian, Federal, Greek Revival, Italianate, American Foursquare, and a variety of common eighteenth-, nineteenth-, and twentieth-century forms.

Transportation is the reason for Breezewood, as well, but of a much more recent vintage. Known variably as "The Town of Motels," "The Travelers' Oasis," and "The Gateway to the South," Breezewood was built with one purpose in mind—serving the traveler. U.S. Highway 30, an

The Lincoln Highway winds its course to McConnellsburg in this vintage postcard.

FACING PAGE:

The restored Compass Inn Museum, built in 1799, was once a stagecoach stop and is now listed on the National Register of Historic Places. It is located in Laughlintown, which lies on the Lincoln Highway near Ligonier.

LEFT:

The bell tower of the United Methodist Church in Mann's Choice, west of Bedford, was built in 1882.

BELOW:

A picturesque red barn and farm wagon sit on a hilltop in Newburg.

interchange for the Pennsylvania Turnpike, and Interstate 70 all came to the small village of about one hundred residents, and following them were the major motel chains, fast food restaurants, and travel-related local businesses. The first such business to open in Breezewood was the Gateway Motel and Restaurant, built in 1941, just after the opening of the turnpike. Try to visit Breezewood at night. The approach, through a mostly dark countryside to a mini-Vegas of neon, is a spectacle you won't soon forget.

Bedford is home to one of the largest fall festivals in the state. The celebration runs the first two weekends in October each year and includes activities like an antique car parade, craft fair, quilt exhibit, juried fine arts exhibit, and much more. The town is also home to Bedford Springs, which from the early 1800s into the early 1900s was one of the premier resorts in the country. A sprawling antebellum-style hotel that once housed the presidents and movie stars who came to soak in the curative waters of the spring, has since declined into disrepair and decay. On the west edge of town, Old Bedford Village is a collection of more than forty reproduction and authentic log, stone, and frame buildings moved to the site from all over Bedford County. Each building boasts a collection of unique artifacts that tells about some aspect of early American life in the county and the state.

WOODCOCK VALLEY
THE APPALACHIAN MOUNTAINS AND RAYSTOWN LAKE

THE ROUTE

Take Pennsylvania Highway 26 north from Everett to Huntingdon.

The Woodcock Valley lies in the heart of the ridge and valley province of the Appalachian Mountains. Our route will carry us through the center of one of those valleys, where tall mountains rise on both sides. Mixed deciduous forests hold the ridge tops, while forests of maple, pine, and hemlock occupy the valleys.

Warriors Path State Park, south of Saxton, is a wonderful spot to explore the region's natural areas. The 349-acre park stands near the famous path once used by Iroquois warriors. The Iroquois used this trail regularly to move south in raids and wars with other Native American tribes and later with European settlers. The Captain Philips Memorial, just off Pennsylvania Highway 26, north of Saxton, marks the site where Native Americans massacred ten frontier militiamen in 1780. The state park, occupying a long finger of land between two meandering bends of the Raystown Branch of the Juniata River, holds a unique habitat of wetlands and weathered shale cliffs.

A valley to the southeast, with numerous side-road connections into the Woodcock Valley, features Raystown Lake, the primary drawing card for this region. The Army Corps of Engineers built the eighty-three-hundred-acre lake in 1975, over the spot where a much smaller dam had impounded the Raystown Branch of the Juniata River since 1907.

The remains of the previous dam rest at the bottom of Raystown Lake, as does the birthplace homestead of a Pennsylvania governor and one of the state's most prolific archaeological sites. Martin Grove Brumbaugh, governor of Pennsylvania from 1915 to 1919, was born in 1862 on a farmstead overlooking the Raystown Branch. Sheep Rock Shelter, discovered along the Raystown Branch in 1957, produced more than eighty thousand artifacts of ancient Native Americans before digging was halted in 1968.

The 118 miles of shoreline around Raystown Lake is largely wild and natural. The Army Corps owns practically all twenty-one thousand acres of it and has provided recreational facilities and allowed concessions to grow at only a few points. Seven Points Marina is the largest marina in Pennsylvania, with 513 wet and 287 dry slips for boats. Lake Raystown Resort is not far behind, with a 650-slip marina. Boat rentals, tours, and cruises are available.

Towns all through the Woodcock Valley reflect the very strong economic influence of Raystown Lake, in the form of fishing guides, boat sales and services, sporting goods stores, and a diversity of restaurants that only tourism dollars can support in small towns. It's difficult to imagine how different the human landscape of these communities would be without the presence of the huge recreational facility.

Juniata College, based in Huntingdon at the end of our tour, maintains a Raystown Field Station on a 365-acre reserve at the lake. Used by a wide range of students and faculty in their research, the station maintains long-term projects like a bird banding station and a water quality analysis laboratory. The school is a Church of the Brethren–affiliated college with about thirteen hundred students and was founded in 1876. As with many college towns, Huntingdon has gained many cultural and artistic offerings from the presence of the college.

Huntingdon was a very early settlement by the standards of this region. The original town was laid out by the Reverend William Smith in 1767, just thirteen years after this region was purchased from the Native Americans. Smith, head of the College of Philadelphia (today the University of Pennsylvania), was an enthusiastic speculator in frontier lands.

Growth of the new community on the unsettled frontier was slow until the 1780s, when settlers began to rush in. Many of Huntingdon's original houses were log while some were made of brick and stone. A few of the latter still exist along Penn Street, as do some of the more substantial brick residences built in the mid-nineteenth century.

PART VI

LAND OF TRANSITIONS:
THE SOUTHWEST

Shadows fall on the front porch of a newsprint company in Roaring Spring, south of Altoona on Highway 36.

A field of sunflowers brightens an Indiana County roadside.

Much of the rugged, mountainous, southwestern region of Pennsylvania is closer to what a traveler expects to encounter in West Virginia than in the Keystone State. Towering mountain peaks rise sharply from deep valleys, coursed by whitewater-packed rivers and streams.

Communities of various vintages, from early settlement to coal-mining and railroading booms, huddle in those valleys. It's mostly a region of small towns and villages, but it's also arranged around Pittsburgh, the state's second-largest city and an example of positive movement from a base dependent on heavy industry to one that flourishes in electronics, communications, and finance.

Natural wonders also abound along our routes. Mount Davis, the tallest point in the entire state, can be found here, as can the Youghiogheny River—the wildest waterway in Pennsylvania—and Raccoon Creek State Park's unique communities of wildflowers.

THE ALLEGHENY PLATEAU
ALTOONA TO INDIANA

THE ROUTE

From Altoona, take Pennsylvania Highway 36 west and north, Township Road 551 west to Hastings, and State Route 4016 west to Northern Cambria. Follow Pennsylvania Highway 271 south to Nicktown, Route 553 west to Penn Run, Township Routes 758 and 686 north to Clymer, and Route 286 southwest to Indiana.

Remnants of Pennsylvania's age of heavy industry, railroad transportation, and soft coal mining stand in nearly every city and small town of the Allegheny Plateau. The rolling hills of the plateaus were settled by thousands of people who migrated into the area for the abundant jobs created by those industries.

Altoona was built in 1849 by the Pennsylvania Railroad, the largest railroad ever in existence, to service locomotives as they pulled long trains back and forth across the Allegheny Mountains. As the railroad grew, so did Altoona. By the early 1900s, it was the biggest construction and research facility for locomotives and trains in the world. More than seventeen thousand people worked in the shops of the Altoona Works. They produced more than sixty-seven hundred locomotives, as well as other rail equipment.

The famed Horseshoe Curve, built in 1845 to move trains through the previously impenetrable Allegheny Mountains, was responsible for much of what Altoona became. Hundreds of laborers carved the 2,375 feet of track bed along the slopes of the Alleghenys, rising through a 220 degree arc that moved trains 122 feet higher from west to east. The only change in the original construction was the movement of the tracks six inches farther apart to allow for the passage of larger trains. So important to the east-west flow of men and material was the Horseshoe Curve that is was third on Hitler's list of targets for Nazi saboteurs in the United States during World War II. The curve was never attacked, having been put under military guard until the saboteurs were captured. The original Horseshoe Curve is today a national historic site. The name has been borrowed by the city's AA baseball team, the Altoona Curve, and the history of all this is on display in the Altoona Railroaders Memorial Museum.

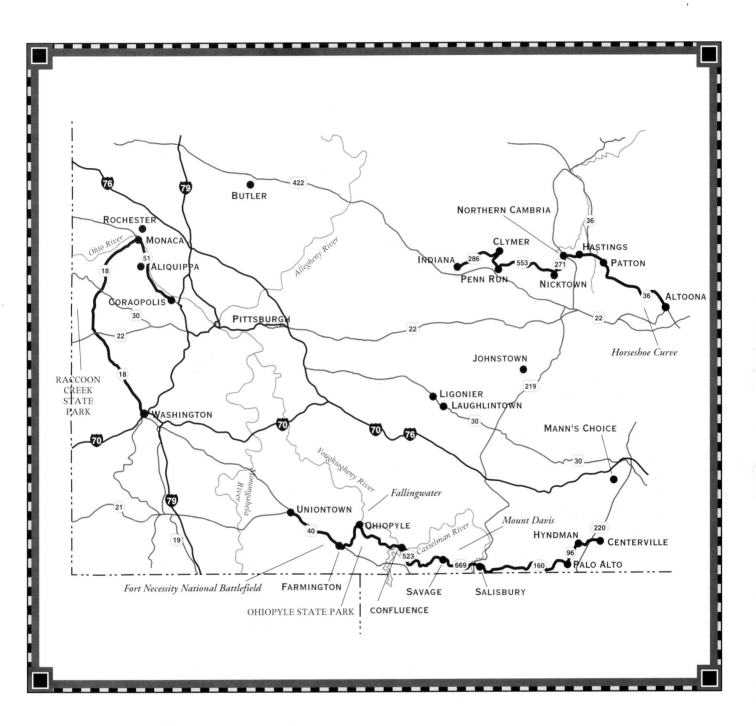

BUTLER
422
76
79
ROCHESTER
Ohio River
MONACA
51
ALIQUIPPA
18
CORAOPOLIS
30
22
PITTSBURGH
Allegheny River
NORTHERN CAMBRIA
36
CLYMER
HASTINGS
INDIANA
286
553
271
PATTON
PENN RUN
NICKTOWN
36
ALTOONA
22
Horseshoe Curve
22
JOHNSTOWN
18
RACCOON
CREEK
STATE
PARK
WASHINGTON
70
219
LIGONIER
LAUGHLINTOWN
30
MANN'S CHOICE
70
70
76
30
21
Monongahela River
Youghiogheny River
Fallingwater
Mount Davis
HYNDMAN
220
CENTERVILLE
79
UNIONTOWN
40
OHIOPYLE
Casselman River
96
PALO ALTO
19
523
669
160
Fort Necessity National Battlefield
FARMINGTON
SAVAGE
SALISBURY
OHIOPYLE STATE PARK
CONFLUENCE

ABOVE:

A classic Mail Pouch barn languishes in a Somerset County pasture.

RIGHT:

This overlook in southwestern Pennsylvania provides a beautiful view of the valley below.

The Horseshoe Curve, pictured in this 1934 photograph, allowed trains to pass through the Allegheny Mountains. (Library of Congress)

Another historic site in Altoona is Lakemont Park. Opened as a trolley park in 1894, it's the eighth-oldest amusement park in the United States. Its restored Leap-the-Dips ride is the world's oldest roller coaster.

As in many small towns of the region, coal mining was a major employer for the men of Patton. However, beginning in 1895, the small community provided the workforce for the Patton Clay Manufacturing Company, which became one of the largest clay manufacturers in the world. Clay products from the Patton works were used in many international projects, including the Panama Canal. Today, the Brickwood Housing Development occupies the former site of the clay plant.

Clymer also saw its origins in the coal industry but gained its few minutes of national fame in 1994, when Saul Knight, of West Virginia, made a telephone call to the town's Borough Hall. "Rumor has it that there is a Clymer, Pennsylvania. If so, let's have a reunion of the U.S.S. *George Clymer* in Clymer," he said, and that is what they did later that year. The Borough of Clymer and the U.S.S. *George Clymer* were both named for George Clymer, a signer of the Declaration of Independence and the Constitution of the United States. The ship was built in 1940 as a passenger ship, purchased by the Navy, and commissioned as a World War II troop transport. The town remembers the event, the ship, and the sailors with artifacts on display in the borough office.

At the western end of our tour stands Indiana, a vibrant town complete with a university and a strong and varied business district. The one thing that any visitor takes away from Indiana, however, is a memory of Jimmy Stewart.

The famous actor was born and raised in Indiana, and the town has taken that fact to heart. The Jimmy Stewart Statue on the lawn of the courthouse at the corner of Eighth and Philadelphia Streets was dedicated and unveiled by Stewart on May 21, 1983, in honor of his seventy-fifth

birthday. Across Philadelphia Street, a sundial marks the location of the former J. M. Stewart & Sons Hardware, where Alex Stewart once displayed his son's Oscar and other memorabilia. The James M. Stewart Museum is located on the third floor of the Indiana Free Library Building on Philadelphia Street. (Another collection of Stewart-related items is held elsewhere in town by the Historical and Genealogical Society of Indiana County.) Travel east on Philadelphia Street, turn left onto Jimmy Stewart Boulevard, proceed one block, and you'll arrive at the base of the long set of concrete steps that leads up to Stewart's boyhood home, still a private residence today.

THE SOUTHERN MOUNTAINS
OHIOPYLE STATE PARK AND THE YOUGHIOGHENY RIVER GORGE

Rugged is the word that best describes the mountains of southwestern Pennsylvania. High peaks, deep valleys, and rushing waters slicing down through gnarled gorges all lend a rustic and wild beauty to this route.

The 19,052-acre Ohiopyle State Park best captures the essence of the region. More than fourteen miles of the Youghiogheny (yaw-ki-gay-nee) River Gorge cuts through the park, offering some of the top whitewater boating in the eastern half of the United States. Cucumber Falls races through the Cucumber Run Ravine, which is seasonally blanketed with wildflowers and flowering rhododendron. Ferncliff Peninsula, formed by a great horseshoe bend in the river, is a unique natural habitat for botanical rarities, particularly wildflower species more common to the south.

Our route begins in a much more civilized part of the region, in the borough of Uniontown, just far enough from Pittsburgh to serve as a commercial hub for the area. From 1870 to 1970, Uniontown was the center of

THE ROUTE

Beginning in Uniontown, take U.S. Highway 40 southeast, Township Road 798 north, Township Road 415 east, and State Route 2011 north to Ohiopyle. From there, follow State Route 2012 south and then east to Confluence and continue southeast on Pennsylvania Highway 523 and east on State Route 2004 to Savage. Take State Route 2002 southeast and Pennsylvania Highway 669 east to Salisbury. Continue east on State Route 2010, Township Road 313, Pennsylvania Highway 160, State Route 2013, and State Route 3002 to Palo Alto. Drive north on Pennsylvania Highway 96 to Hyndman, and from there take an unmarked gravel road east to Centerville.

The Old Indiana County Court-house is on the National Register of Historic Places. Pictured here is a close-up of its clock tower.

Indiana County War Memorial is also located at the Indiana court-house. The memorial, which lists over fifteen hundred names, honors the men and women of the area who have died fighting for their country.

Jimmy Stewart, the Academy Award–winning actor who starred in such films as It's a Wonderful Life *and* Harvey *was born in Indiana, Pennsylvania. He is remembered there with a museum and a statue, which stands on the lawn of the county courthouse.*

ABOVE RIGHT:

In 1837, this stone storage building was constructed for the Allegheny furnace, which processed iron ore. It is located on Highway 36 in Altoona.

LEFT:

Pumpkins are lined up for sale at this roadside stand in southwestern Pennsylvania.

FRANK LLOYD WRIGHT'S FALLINGWATER

Just north of Ohiopyle State Park, straddling a waterfall of Bear Run, the traveler will find Fallingwater, one of the most famous works of one of America's most influential architects.

Frank Lloyd Wright, who lived from 1867 to 1959, designed the home, which became a symbol for the public of unusual trends in modern architecture even as it was being built in the 1930s. Designed for Pittsburgh department store owner Edgar J. Kaufmann, Fallingwater was built directly over a waterfall that was a favorite spot of the family. The structure was made of sandstone quarried on the site and positioned by local craftsmen.

Fallingwater, which today is owned by the Western Pennsylvania Conservancy and open for public visits, was just one mark in Wright's career, which included innovations like the Prairie style. Porches and terraces expand the interior of a Prairie home outside into the surrounding environment, giving the structure the feeling that it grew from the world around it.

Frank Lloyd Wright is one of the United States's most respected architects.

an industry based on extracting coke, a coal residue used for fuel, from an area three to four miles wide and about forty miles long, known as the Connellsville Coke Region. The Coal and Coke Heritage Center at Penn State's Fayette Campus in Uniontown traces that era through a collection of artifacts and oral histories.

Uniontown has the standard VFW Home along Main Street, as do so many communities across Pennsylvania, but with a huge variation. The Uniontown home stands on the site of birthplace and boyhood home of General George C. Marshall, for whom the Marshall Plan of recovery for Europe in the wake of World War II was named. Under that plan, from 1948 to 1951, the United States contributed more than $13 billion in various forms of assistance to the countries of free Europe.

George Washington fought here—at Fort Necessity near Farmington, that is. In fact, the twenty-two-year-old colonel lost his first battle here at the start of the French and Indian War in 1754. The nine-hundred-acre Fort Necessity National Battlefield traces these historic events and more in three separate sites, extensive collections, and reconstructed facilities, such as the fort itself and the Mount Washington Tavern.

Laurel Caverns, a 430-acre geological park featuring Pennsylvania's largest cave, lies just outside Farmington. Unlike the other public caves of the state, Laurel's geology has not created any stalactite or stalagmite formations. It compensates for that in the magnitude of its rooms and passageways.

Confluence, where steep mountains touch roaring rivers, gets its name from its location at the convergence of the Youghiogheny River, Casselman River, and Laurel Hill Creek. The rugged and remote landscape and the rushing whitewater have made the borough a center for outdoor recreation enthusiasts. Several of Pennsylvania's top resorts have located nearby, including the sprawling and diverse Seven Springs Mountain Resort. Passing through Confluence is the Great Allengheny Passage, a biking and hiking trail connecting Cumberland, Maryland, and Pittsburgh, which will be the longest rails-to-trails project in the East when its full 152 miles are completed.

East of Confluence, Mount Davis soars to the highest point in Pennsylvania, 3,213 feet above sea level. The easily accessed peak towers over the surrounding landscape, which includes Deer Valley Lake (2,654 feet above sea level) and High Point Lake (2,480 feet above sea level), and provides a fantastic view of the region.

AMERICA'S FIRST FRONTIER
THE OHIO RIVER VALLEY

The Ohio River Valley, the first several miles of which we follow on this route, is often referred to as the First American West. Long before the bison of the Great Plains and the peaks of the Rockies became the symbols of the West, intrepid pioneers and dogged settlers were making their way out of Pittsburgh and down the Ohio River to unsettled lands east of the Mississippi.

The French explorer Robert Cavelier Sieur de LaSalle reached the Ohio River in 1669, and the European powers began tapping into the natural resources of the region in the early 1700s. However, the region really rose to significance in the 1750s as the British and the French fought for control of the important trade route. The first settlement was established in 1749 by the British Ohio Company of Virginia at the site of modern-day Pittsburgh. The fort was captured and changed hands numerous times, existing as the British Fort Pitt at the end of the French and Indian War. At the end of that conflict in 1763, the river was established as part of the British Empire, but settlement there was prohibited and not opened until 1787, after the United States had won the Revolutionary War.

Drive north on Pennsylvania Highway 51 from Coraopolis to Monaca. From there, follow Pennsylvania Highway 18 west and south to Washington.

Canoeists shoot the falls on the Youghiogheny River in Ohiopyle State Park.

ABOVE:

The Youghiogheny River invites all kinds of recreation seekers. Here, anglers try for a bite near Confluence in Somerset County.

RIGHT:

A field of black-eyed Susans grows beside a Bedford County backroad.

Steel production has historically been one of Pittsburgh's biggest industries. This vintage photograph shows men at the Pittsburgh steel works cleaning and repairing a ladle, which was able to hold about fifteen tons of melted iron.

While settlement of the region began many years earlier, it greatly increased with the Northwest Ordinance of 1787, which established the new Northwest Territory. By the time Lewis and Clark moved their Corps of Discovery through this part of the Ohio River in the fall of 1803, plenty of villages had sprung to full life along the river.

Although the official Voyage of Discovery did not begin for several months, Lewis and Clark did camp at two points along our route after they left Pittsburgh. On September 2, 1803, in one of their first nights out of Pittsburgh, the expedition camped on Hog Island near Aliquippa. The next night, they camped near today's Montgomery Dam, which is the point at which our route turns south and away from the Ohio River.

The 981-mile-long Ohio River begins in Pittsburgh at the confluence of the Allegheny and Monongahela Rivers, flowing northwest before turning for its southwesterly run to the Mississippi River at Cairo, Illinois. Until the opening of the Erie Canal in 1825, the Ohio River was the main route to the West and the main route for bringing the agricultural production of the West to the East. Even today, the Ohio is second only to the Mississippi for transporting cargo, moving about two hundred million tons per year. Coal accounts for nearly half that total, with agricultural products, chemicals, gravel, petroleum products, and steel products making up the bulk of the rest.

The Ohio River Valley remains one of the most populated and industrialized river valleys in the United States, obvious in the first leg of our tour from Coraopolis north to Monaca. However, after we turn south near Montgomery Ferry, we soon find ourselves in a hilly countryside of small towns and natural wonders.

The 7,323-acre Raccoon Creek State Park sits right in the middle of the rural landscape just outside Pittsburgh. Started as a National Park Service recreational demonstration area in the 1930s, the park is now one of the largest in the state park system. A highlight of the park is the Wildflower Reserve, a 314-acre area that contains one of the most unique stands of wildflowers in western Pennsylvania. More than five hundred species of flowering plants thrive along the five miles of trails. Peak bloom periods are late April through May and August through early September.

Breaking with the natural sense of the area, Star Lake Amphitheater near the intersection of Pennsylvania Highway 18 and U.S. Highway 22 brings some of the biggest names in music to the its stage. In addition to the massive, open-air performance grounds, numerous restaurants and music-related businesses have taken up residence around the site to accommodate the huge crowds drawn there throughout the spring and summer.

Down the road in Washington, the end of our route, the Pennsylvania Trolley Museum returns us again to a gentler time, complete with a three-mile ride on an authentic trolley. In the early 1940s, the museum's founders launched an effort to save some of the old streetcars that were disappearing from the scene. By 1949 they had acquired their first trolley, a small four-wheeled model about to be scrapped by the Pittsburgh Railways Company. They bought the Washington interurban trolley line from the same company in 1953 to house their growing collection of trolley cars.

ABOVE:
In the town of Monaca, a bridge crosses to Rochester over the junction of the Beaver and Ohio Rivers.

FACING PAGE, TOP:
This 1950s Philadelphia trolley car can be found at the Pennsylvania Trolley Museum in Washington. Conductor Harry Hohman says, "Come aboard!"

FACING PAGE, BOTTOM:
The Pennsylvania Trolley Museum preserves trolleys that may have otherwise been destroyed. Pictured here is the interior of a vintage Philadelphia trolley car.

INDEX

SUGGESTED READING

Bailey, Bill, et al. *Pennsylvania State Parks*. Saginaw, Mich.: Glovebox Guidebooks of America, 1996.

Deleon, Clark. *Pennsylvania Curiosities*. Guilford, Conn.: Globe Pequot Press, 2001.

Miller, Joanne. *Moon Handbooks: Pennsylvania,* 2nd edition. Emeryville, Calif.: Avalon Travel Publishing, 2001.

Ostertag, Rhonda and George. *Scenic Driving Pennsylvania*. Guilford, Conn.: Falcon Publishing, Inc., 2002.

Paul, Lewis M. *Discovering Pennsylvania*. Beaverton, Ore.: American Products Publishing Company, 2001.

Paulsen, Emily and Faith. *Fun With the Family in Pennsylvania,* 4th edition. Guilford, Conn.: Globe Pequot Press, 2002.

Pennsylvania Atlas & Gazetteer, 7th edition. Yarmouth, Maine: DeLorme Publishing, 2000.

Perloff, Susan. *Pennsylvania: Off The Beaten Path,* 6th edition. Guilford, Conn.: Globe Pequot Press, 2002.

Root, Douglas. *Compass American Guides: Pennsylvania*. New York: Fodor's Travel Publications, Inc., 2000.

Schneck, Marcus. *Country Towns of Pennsylvania,* 2nd edition. New York: McGraw-Hill/Contemporary Books, 1999.

Black-and-white Holstein cows graze in a marshy field on a Chester County farm near Honey Brook.

ABOUT THE AUTHOR AND PHOTOGRAPHER

Native Pennsylvanian Marcus Schneck has written about the Keystone State, travel, and the outdoors since 1978. He is outdoor editor and environmental contributor at the *Patriot-News* in Harrisburg, Pennsylvania, and publications director at *Keystone Conservationist* in Camp Hill. His work has appeared in nearly every Pennsylvania-focused magazine, including *Pennsylvania Magazine*, *Northwoods Journal*, *Pennsylvania Wildlife*, *Keystone Conservationist*, and *Pennsylvania Game News*. He also is the author of more than two dozen books.

(Photograph © Jill Caravan)

Glenn Davis of Honey Brook, Pennsylvania, has always loved the outdoors. While working in the environmental field, he became interested in photography, pursued it as a hobby, and in 1989 started Davis Photographic Specialties. As a professional photographer, he focuses on natural history subjects and commercial advertising. Davis has been a featured guest on the *Call of the Outdoors* television program. Articles on his work have been featured in *Shutterbug* and *Commercial Image* magazines, and his photographs have appeared on the covers of *Audubon* and *Country Journal*, in *National Geographic*, Sierra Club calendars, *Natural History*, Hallmark greeting cards, *Pennsylvania*, and numerous other national publications.

(Photograph © Darlene Davis)

RK 52 .M46 2010

Miller, Chris H.,

Infection control and
management of hazardous

INFECTION
CONTROL

and Management of Hazardous Materials
for the Dental Team

Library
Camden County College
Blackwood, NJ

WITHDRAWN

WITHDRAWN!